TEACHING MATHEMATICS 5 to 11

CROOM HELM TEACHING 5–13 SERIES
Edited by Colin Richards, formerly of the School of
Education, Leicester University

Assessment in Primary and Middle Schools
Marten Shipman

Organising Learning in the Primary School Classroom
Joan Dean

*Development, Experience and Curriculum in Primary
Education*
W.A.L. Blyth

Place and Time with Children Five to Nine
Joan Blyth

Children and Art Teaching
Keith Gentle

Teaching Craft Design and Technology 5–13
Peter H.M. Williams

Teaching Mathematics 5 to 11

DAVID LUMB

CROOM HELM
London & Sydney

NICHOLS PUBLISHING COMPANY
New York

© 1987 David Lumb
Croom Helm Ltd, Provident House, Burrell Row,
Beckenham, Kent BR3 1AT
Croom Helm Australia, 44-50 Waterloo Road,
North Ryde, 2113, New South Wales

British Library Cataloguing in Publication Data

Lumb, D.
    Teaching Mathematics 5 to 11. — (Croom Helm teaching
    5-13 series)
    1. Mathematics — Study and teaching
    (Elementary)
    I. Title
    372.7'3044   QA135.5
    ISBN 0-7099-4118-8
    ISBN 0-7099-4128-5 Pbk

First published in the United States of America in 1987 by
Nichols Publishing Company,
Post Office Box 96, New York, NY 10024

Library of Congress Cataloging-in-Publication Data

Lumb, David.
    Teaching mathematics, 5–11.

    (Teaching 5–13)
    1. Mathematics — Study and teaching (Primary)
2. Mathematics — Study and teaching (Elementary)
I. Title: Teaching mathematics, five thru eleven.
II. Series: Croom Helm teaching 5–13.
QA135.5.L85 1987   372.7   87–5633
ISBN 0-89397-274-6
ISBN 0-89397-275-4 (pbk.)

Printed and bound in Great Britain
by Billing & Sons Limited, Worcester.

Contents

Series Foreword

Teaching 5–13 is a series of books intended to foster the professional development of teachers in primary and middle schools. The series is being published at a time when there are growing demands on teachers to demonstrate increasing levels of professional understanding and competence. Although the importance of personal qualities and social skills in successful teaching is acknowledged, the series is based on the premisses that the enhancement of teacher competence and judgement in curricular and organisational matters is the major goal of pre-service and in-service teacher education and that this enhancement is furthered, not by the provision of recipes to be applied in any context, but by the application of practical principles for the organisation and management of learning, and for the planning, implementation and evaluation of curricula. The series aims to help teachers and trainee teachers to think out for themselves ways of tackling the problems which confront them in their own particular range of circumstances. It does this by providing two kinds of books: those which focus on a particular area of the primary or middle-school curriculum and those which discuss general issues germane to any area of the curriculum.

1

Introduction

Mathematics is one of the most important parts of the primary curriculum. There is, however, no general agreement on crucial issues relating to just how the subject should be taught, and many teachers are confused by the bewildering array of materials and ideas with which they are bombarded but which they have little time to assimilate.

This book attempts to survey some of the current issues of mathematics teaching in primary schools. Chapters 2 and 3 examine the various reports and suggestions for change that have been drawn up in recent years and discuss the place of mathematics in the primary curriculum. Chapter 4 is devoted to an examination of the mathematical development likely to occur for the child in the primary years. Chapters 5 and 6 look at the problems facing the teacher in trying to accommodate pupils at either end of the ability range: children with learning difficulties and children who show above-average ability in mathematics. Chapters 7 and 8 are concerned with the influence of modern technology on the mathematics taught in the primary school, as seen by the use of the calculator and the microcomputer. Chapter 9 looks at the difficult area of problem-solving and investigation work which is so new to many teachers. Chapters 10, 11 and 12 focus on a number of matters connected with the organisation of mathematics teaching in the school, consider how decisions are made with regard to the choice of a suitable textbook scheme, and review various issues related to the assessment of mathematical progress. The appendix suggests some ways in which a local authority can provide resource support for a primary school.

2

Cockcroft and All That

1982 was a year of great significance for teachers of mathematics. *Mathematics Counts*,[1] the report of the Committee of Inquiry into the Teaching of Mathematics in Schools under the chairmanship of Dr W.H. Cockcroft, was published. The longest chapter in the report — and the most authoritative ever to be provided on the teaching of mathematics — was devoted to the primary school.

After acknowledging that the vast majority of primary teachers are acutely aware of their responsibility to provide children with a solid mathematical foundation, the report suggests that many teachers would welcome specific guidance in the task.

Is this cry for help and guidance anything new? In order to answer this question and place the Cockcroft Report in context, it will be helpful to briefly summarise the main recommendations affecting the primary teacher and then compare these with the recommendations made in other recent reports.

MATHEMATICS COUNTS

Attention is given to the general reasons for teaching mathematics, with an emphasis placed on the power of the subject to communicate itself through its concise, unambiguous nature and its ability to represent, explain and predict. In the learning of mathematics the effects of variation of speed, attainment and rate of learning are discussed. The fact that mathematics is a difficult subject both to teach and to learn is boldly acknowledged.

In the section on teaching methods, three distinct elements are identified: facts and skills; conceptual structures; and general strategies and appreciation. These need to be organised accordingly. Mathematics teaching should provide opportunities for six kinds of activity: exposition by the teacher; discussion between teacher and pupils and among the pupils themselves; appropriate practical work; consolidation and practice; problem-solving, including applications to everyday situations; and investigational work.

The Committee applauded the broadening of the primary mathematics curriculum over the past 20 years to take in a greater understanding of number and to include work on measurement, shape and space, graphical representation and simple logic. It was felt that this has led to an improvement in children's understanding of, and attitude to, mathematics. The view that primary schools pay insufficient attention to the developing of computational skills is rejected. Young children should not be expected to progress too quickly to written work. The importance of mental and oral work in the early stages of learning is stressed.

Explicit statements are made concerning the importance of language in mathematics. This is placed centrally in the learning of mathematics as a tool of thinking and as a means of communication.

Suggestions are made with reference to the special needs of pupils whose level of attainment is either particularly high or particularly low, and attention is drawn to the wide range of attainment which can be expected among young children of the same age. A 'seven-year difference' in the age at which pupils show an understanding of certain topics is identified. One example quoted is that of writing down the number which is one greater than 6399. This task can be performed by an 'average' child at the age of eleven, but there are some fourteen-year-olds who cannot do it and some seven-year-olds who can.

It is recommended that the time allocated to mathematics should be about five hours a week, and that even older children should do no more than one hour at a time. Mental work should be undertaken for brief periods only. Also, one teacher should be given the responsibility of co-ordinating mathematics within the school.

The Committee felt that primary teachers should know how to use the calculator and allow their pupils to use it where appropriate, while stating that it remains essential that children should acquire a grasp of basic number facts. The use of computers as an aid to teaching mathematics is recommended.

OTHER REPORTS

The broadening of the primary mathematics curriculum and the promotion of methods which involve learning through understanding rather than by rote, as recommended in the Cockcroft Report, are not new. In 1931, the Hadow Report, *The Primary School*,[2] stated: 'The curriculum is to be thought of in terms of activity and experience rather than of knowledge to be acquired and facts to be stored.'

In 1956, the report produced by the Mathematical Association, *The Teaching of Mathematics in Primary Schools*,[3] recommended the following:

> We are convinced that the important thing is to help children to understand mathematical ideas and to recognise the kind of computation, or other thought processes, which a problem situation demands. If a particular child is slow to gain understanding he may well pass through the primary stage before he is ready for formal sums.

The Plowden Report[4] of 1966 quoted statistics to illustrate the point made: 'Instruction in many primary schools continues to bewilder children because it outruns their experience. Even in infant schools time is sometimes spent in teaching written sums before children are ready to understand what they are doing.'

The National Child Development Study survey shows that 17 per cent of children start doing sums before the age of five and a half. (This study is based on a national sample of children born in one week in 1958. For further information see the Plowden Report.)

Curriculum Bulletin Number 1: Mathematics in Primary Schools,[5] published in 1965 by the Schools Council, requested every teacher to ensure that his or her pupils experienced the joy of discovery to be found in mathematics and to provide them with work in shape, space, graphical representation and measurement as well as number.

It is significant that since the 1950s there has been a gradual change of name from 'number' to 'arithmetic' to 'mathematics' as the curriculum has broadened. Public opinion in recent years may have caused some primary teachers to wonder if they were correct in developing a broader approach to the subject and to question the wisdom of this claim made in *Curriculum Bulletin No. 1*:

> We can say with complete assurance, every teacher who embarks on a programme which will enable children to make their own discoveries in mathematics will share to their utmost their children's enjoyment of mathematics and their increasing confidence in their own powers.

If this is the case, then the Cockcroft Report should provide the teacher with complete assurance.

A FUNDAMENTAL QUESTION

The kind of mathematics teaching recommended in the Cockcroft Report is firmly based on the thinking that lies behind these other reports. This thinking has been supported and developed by projects such as the Nuffield Primary Mathematics Project and has been the subject of numerous in-service and initial training courses. Countless primary guidelines have been produced by local authorities. (See *Mathematics in School*, vol. 11 no. 5.[6]) The two HMI guideline documents, *Mathematics 5–11*[7] and *Mathematics from 5 to 16*[8] are full of similar recommendations.

A fundamental question arises from the Cockcroft Report. Given all this emphasis over the last 30 years on a broad primary curriculum based on understanding, discovery and practical work, why should the messages have needed restating so emphatically in 1981? Had the messages not been heard, not been understood, not been followed up — or had they simply been rejected?

These questions can be answered to some extent by examining the teaching of mathematics in primary schools in England and Wales as found by Her Majesty's Inspectors in some of their recent reports.

HMI REPORTS

In *Primary Education in England,*[9] published in 1978, children were reported to be spending too much time undertaking repetitive practice of processes they had already mastered in a third of the classes visited. Practical activities were confined to repetitive measurement and weighing in over 50 per cent of the classes.

In *Education 5–9,*[10] published in 1982, the mathematical diet of many young children is severely criticised. In 80 per cent of the schools inspected, mathematical skills were practised in isolation, with the bulk of the work based either on self-contained, commercially produced schemes or on graded work-cards made in the school. The main element in many schools was computation, with the sole aim of reaching a certain standard of efficiency in abstract calculation. Younger children were just as likely to be practising mathematical skills in isolation as the older ones within the age range.

In *9–13 Middle Schools,*[11] published in 1983, it was found that too much time was being spent on the routine practice of skills, particularly by the less able. Pupils were often proficient in the set rules but unable to apply them in unfamiliar situations. Considerable emphasis was often placed on computational practice devoid of application, and this was particularly the case with average and more able children.

In only 50 per cent of the schools observed was practical work regarded as an important aspect of mathematics, and only then, in some cases, by a minority of teachers in the school. The practical activities suggested in textbooks were frequently either omitted or curtailed, especially in the work with older pupils.

Contrast these comments with this extract from an HMI report from the last century:

> The accuracy of the work in Standards I and II is all that can be desired, and in many cases marvellous; at the same time the oral test shows that the children are working in the dark. For these standards, at least, far too much time is given to the mechanical part of the subject. The result of this unintelligent teaching shows itself in the inability of the upper standards to solve very simple problems. (1895)[12]

So little seems to have changed, in some schools, since 1895.

It is therefore hardly surprising that the Cockcroft Report found it necessary to repeat the messages of understanding, discovery and practical work so emphatically.

Many primary teachers would claim to be undertaking some practical work in their teaching of mathematics. There may, however, be an underlying misconception related to what practical work in mathematics actually involves. To be fair to the primary teacher, it must be admitted that the Cockcroft Report fails to describe practical work adequately, and the term is used in a variety of contexts. Those teachers with a limited view of such work, who base their teaching almost entirely on the practice of arithmetical skills, may believe themselves to be carrying out the kind of practical work recommended and thus see little need to develop their teaching style. Chapter 9 will be of interest to such teachers.

ASSESSMENT OF PERFORMANCE UNIT

The results of the Assessment of Performance Unit (APU)[13] raise some interesting questions concerning the actual level of understanding reached by many primary children in their mathematical thinking. The written tests used with eleven-year-olds show how superficial the grasp of arithmetical processes can be. For example, in response to the item asking for the fractions $\frac{1}{2}$, $\frac{5}{8}$, and $\frac{1}{4}$ to be placed in order of size, with the smallest first, the following responses were obtained:

$\frac{1}{4}$	$\frac{1}{2}$	$\frac{5}{8}$	36%
$\frac{5}{8}$	$\frac{1}{4}$	$\frac{1}{2}$	36%
$\frac{1}{2}$	$\frac{1}{4}$	$\frac{5}{8}$	10%
$\frac{5}{8}$	$\frac{1}{2}$	$\frac{1}{4}$	1%
Other			14%
Omit			3%

Almost two out of five eleven-year-olds appear to be ignoring the numerator, concluding that any number of eighths is smaller than any number of quarters.

With the question $\frac{1}{2} + \frac{1}{3}$, 24 per cent used a wrong rule, adding the numerators and adding the denominators, to obtain

$$\frac{1+1}{2+3} = \frac{2}{5}.$$

Only 34 per cent were able to give a correct answer to the question 5.07 − 1.3.

A detailed study of *Retrospective Report: A Review of Performance in Mathematics, 1978 to 1982*[14] will provide further examples of this tenuous level of understanding in other areas of mathematics. It also appears from the findings of the APU that children's thinking in practical situations is often more advanced than their skill in performing abstract calculations.

It is clear that much needs to be done in the primary school if the following aim, from Cockcroft, is to be achieved:

The primary mathematics curriculum should enrich children's aesthetic and linguistic experience, provide them with the means of exploring their environment and develop their powers of logical thought, in addition to equipping them with the numerical skills which will be a powerful tool for later work and study.

REFERENCES

1. Cockcroft, W.H. (Chairman), *Mathematics Counts*, Report of the Committee of Inquiry into the Teaching of Mathematics in Schools (HMSO, 1982).

2. Hadow Report, The *Education of the Adolescent* (HMSO, 1926).

3. Mathematical Association, *Teaching of Mathematics in Primary Schools* (Bell, 1956).

4. Plowden Report, *Children and their Primary Schools* (HMSO, 1967).

5. Schools Council, *Curriculum Bulletin No. 1: Mathematics in Primary Schools* (HMSO, 1965).

6. Mathematical Association, B. Wilson, 'Primary Guidelines', Two articles in *Mathematics in School*, vol. II, no. 5 (November, 1982) and vol. 13, no. 2 (March 1984).

7. DES, *Mathematics 5–11: A Handbook of Suggestions by HM Inspectors* (HMSO, 1979).

8. DES, *Mathematics from 5 to 16, Curriculum Matters 3*, an HMI series (HMSO, 1985).

9. DES, *Primary Education in England*, a survey by HM Inspectors of Schools (HMSO, 1978).

10. DES, *Education 5–9, An Illustrative Survey of 80 First Schools in England* (HMSO, 1982).

11. DES, *9–13 Middle Schools, A Survey by HM Inspectors of Schools* (HMSO, 1983).

12. McIntosh, A., *When Will They Ever Learn?*, Forum for the Discussion of New Trends in Education, vol. 19, no. 3 (Summer 1977).

13. Assessment of Performance Unit, *Mathematical Development: Primary Survey Report No, 1* (HMSO, 1980).

APU, *Mathematical Development: Primary Survey Report No. 2* (HMSO, 1981).

APU, *Mathematical Development: Primary Survey Report No. 3* (HMSO, 1982).

14. APU, *Retrospective Report: A Review of Performance in Mathematics, 1978 to 1982* (HMSO, 1985).

3

Aims and Objectives

THE PLACE OF MATHEMATICS IN THE CURRICULUM

Today, mathematics is regarded as an essential component of the school curriculum. Literacy and numeracy are assumed to be acquired by all children during their school careers, though this assumption is not always found to be valid in reality and a considerable number of them do leave school at 16 either illiterate or innumerate. The amount of time on the primary school timetable allocated to language work and mathematics reflects the importance which is attached to both these areas.

Mathematics has not always been considered a vital part of formal education. Arithmetic only started to grow in importance on a large scale during the nineteenth century when the appreciation of its usefulness to the community resulted in its rise in esteem. Later in the century, this was followed by mathematics, though the emphasis on the latter seems to have been based more on the supposed usefulness of the subject in developing mental discipline than upon its direct value in any technological or vocational context. Various revolts against the accepted views of mathematical education have occurred since that time. A major revolt occurred in the 1960s, when the whole of the mathematical curriculum was examined very carefully and aspects of modern mathematics were introduced. This was deemed necessary in order to equip children to face the reality of life in the new technological age of the future. This development has been followed more recently by the ripples produced by the publication of the Cockcroft Report.

AIMS AND OBJECTIVES

Many studies have centred around the theme of objectives in the teaching of mathematics. This growth in the interest in objective analysis in mathematics teaching coincided with, and was part of, the general increase in attention to curriculum development. A large number of curriculum programmes have been sponsored by the Schools Council and more recently and to a lesser extent by the School Curriculum Development Committee. Primary Initiatives in Mathematics Education (PRIME), launched in 1986, is the latest of such programmes.

The general principles behind the instigation of programmes of work or new courses can be summarised in the following four stages:

(1) A statement of the programme's aims.

(2) A breakdown of these aims into specific objectives.

(3) An expression of these specific objectives in terms of measurable changes in pupil behaviour. These changes might be the result of some newly acquired knowledge, values, skills, attitudes, types of understanding, etc.

(4) An evaluation of the attainment of these objectives.

Although these stages may seem self-evident, it would be naïve to assume that all learning can be expressed in terms of easily measurable changes in behaviour. It is probably true that the statement of objectives is easier in a subject like mathematics, but it might not always be practicable to express objectives in mathematics in very precise detail. While it is extremely unlikely that two teachers would ever be in total agreement on their respective objectives in teaching mathematics, there should be sufficient agreement about general objectives to make a discussion of these objectives worth while.

Student teachers will increase their understanding of mathematics teaching by examining the aims of the exercise in detail, and experienced teachers will probably find that frequent reminders of the aims of the subject are very useful. It is to be hoped that the educational practices being adopted in the teaching of mathematics within the school do approximate to those suggested by the aims of the course. There is, of course, a danger of losing sight of the aims of the course in attempting to lead children to understand particular concepts. The teacher then tends to proceed intuitively and the theoretical framework for the development remains implicit and unformulated.

The aims suggested here for the teaching of mathematics are grouped into five categories: attitude to and enjoyment of mathematics; mathematical horizons; communication; computation, measurement and shape; and discovery

Naturally these categories will overlap, and connections can be found between individual aims both within and between categories.

Aims for the teaching of mathematics

Attitude and enjoyment

(1) Encourage a favourable attitude to mathematics.

(2) Present mathematics in an interesting and enjoyable way.

(3) Allow the child to be actively engaged in the learning process at both individual and group levels. The pupils will become actively engaged with one another through the group approach.

(4) Create a sense of achievement in the learning of mathematics at each stage and so help the child gain confidence in dealing with the subject. This feeling of confidence must be maintained even if the rate of progress is slow.

Mathematical horizons

(1) Aid the children in their understanding and mastery of the basic concepts and help them to use these basic concepts to progress towards more sophisticated stages of mathematics.

(2) Revise, practise, consolidate and develop a deeper understanding of the concepts, principles and experience already encountered and utilise this in developing newer areas of mathematics.

(3) Show the connection between mathematics and other areas of the school curriculum, and develop the mathematical skills required in these other areas.

(4) Indicate the importance of mathematics in the world today and be aware of the utilitarian aspects of the subject.

(5) Explore the creative and aesthetic aspects of mathematics.

Communication

(1) Encourage the child to communicate both verbally and symbolically.

(2) Allow the children to have opportunities to discuss their work with others.

(3) Foster the ability to record and so provide a sound conceptual framework for developing more sophisticated mathematical ideas.

(4) Develop the child's mathematical vocabulary.

(5) Allow mathematics to develop as a corporate activity involving both the pupils and the teacher.

(6) Develop the child's ability to think clearly and logically with an independence of thought and flexibility of mind.

Computation, measurement and shape

(1) Encourage the child to deal quickly and accurately with the basic rules of arithmetic, but try to apply these rules only to sensible situations.

(2) Introduce the child to different kinds of aid designed for performing mathematical calculations, especially the use of the calculator.

(3) Develop an appreciation of the nature of number, shape and measurement leading to an awareness of the basic structure of mathematics.

Discovery

(1) Lead the child towards meaningful discoveries. This should assist in developing a self-confidence in the subject.

(2) Help the child to make decisions and formulate hypotheses at appropriate levels of sophistication.

(3) Stimulate the child's progress by using experimental and practical methods when appropriate.

(4) Help the children to arrive at mathematical concepts which they are likely to internalise.

4

Mathematical Development

The purpose of this section is to identify a clear development in mathematics through the primary years. This will be done by considering a programme of concepts and skills in number, shape, measurement and representation; but first let us consider briefly the mathematical foundation which must be provided in the early stages of pre-school, nursery and reception work. If this foundation is shaky, the building up of higher-order skills and concepts will be almost impossible.

FOUNDATION

For the very young child the natural environment, together with man-made materials and play equipment, will provide all the opportunities he or she requires for mathematical development. This selection of materials, equipment and activities should be wide, and initially children should be allowed to choose for themselves. The range of experiences should include large toys, large bricks, wet and dry sand, water, clay, painting, constructional toys, a 'home corner' including dressing up, music, movement, books, stories and poetry.

It is important that from the earliest stages children should be allowed to develop their understanding of pattern. They need to handle three-dimensional solids such as large bricks of varying shapes and sizes, to make models from waste materials and to experiment with shapes of all kinds. Children will appreciate symmetry in the world they see around them. At this stage of development the children's activities will be intrinsically valuable from the mathematical point of view and will also be absorbing in the way they enliven, enrich and extend vocabulary. This should be stimulated and extended. When descriptive language arises, teachers can extend learning beyond the confines of mathematics. For example, while recognising the importance of comparisons such as 'heavier than', 'lighter than', the teacher must be quick to respond to the delights of any unusual descriptive language used that relates to weighing. It follows that there are many opportunities to enrich children's vocabulary with regard to colour, texture, form and involvement. The acquisition of this vocabulary plays an important role in the education of children and the development of the powers to discriminate and classify.

Discrimination and classification are fundamental concepts which have, to some extent, become formally identified with the language of sets and the commercial packs of sorting apparatus seen in many classrooms. Many of the opportunities for sorting are artificially created, but in a good environment sorting happens spontaneously. This environment will also provide experience of basic number work without counting or formal measurement being undertaken. Grading toys provide opportunities to put objects in order of size; dressing dolls of different sizes requires the sorting of clothes that fit; putting lids on pans, buttoning coats, putting out cups and saucers, knives and forks, provide ample experience of one-to-one correspondence. Children will need to handle objects which are relatively heavy and light of the same, and different, shapes and sizes.

It is important not to rush children into written work in mathematics before they are ready for it. Children listen to the English language for five years and speak it for about four before we expect them to read and write it. The same is true of mathematics. A child must be allowed ample time to operate with mathematical language before being expected to comprehend written and symbolic forms and before being expected to record his or her understanding on paper.

Children come to school accustomed to solving problems. Number work should not be divorced from problems, as so often happens. Children are not ready to practise sums until they are able to express orally what they are doing. They should not be introduced to symbols until they are capable of conveying orally and pictorially what they mean. When introduced to a type of sum they should meet it in problem form, and when given a sum should be able to suggest a situation from which it has arisen.

Teachers of young children need to be able to observe their pupils and help them to develop ideas. They need to know when a child is indicating intuitively some basic understanding. They must also know when to intervene to assist the child to ensure that he or she is neither forced nor held back. There is, needless to say, a narrow line between intervention and interference, and teachers must be aware of this.

CONCEPTUAL BREAKDOWN

The following summary is intended to indicate the kinds of mathematical topic which should be introduced to children between the ages of four and 13. No indication is given as to which topics should be encountered by a particular age since the rates of development of children should be considered individually. Teachers are left to determine which levels are appropriate for their pupils at which ages.

It is hoped that the breakdown will provide teachers with a useful means of checking their own syllabuses or with a basis for re-planning their own programmes as required. Although some parts of the breakdown follow a certain natural and logical order, other items may be placed in several different kinds of order, all of which are feasible from the developmental point of view. Consequently, within some of the groupings no particular significance should be attached to the ordering of the individual items.

Number

(It is assumed here that calculators will be available).

Basic sorting leading to perception of space, colour and shape

Matching activities

Number names and sequence to six. (Number rhymes are useful here, and later on.)

Recognition of two, three, four and one

Cardinal numbers of sets with one to four objects

Number sequence to ten, always counting actual objects, names, symbols.

Ordinal numbers (first, second, third, etc.)

None, nothing, zero

Patterns made by a collection of objects (conservation). Until the pupils appreciate the conservation principle, little progress will be made with addition and subtraction.

Picture and recognition of numbers

Operations of addition and subtraction ('take away'), using sets of objects

Do not use quick methods at this stage.

The other aspect of subtraction is 'difference between', which should be dealt with separately.

Composition of numbers to six by use of concrete materials. The aim here should be the understanding and not the memorisation of number facts (though, of course, some pupils may remember them) i.e. $3 + 2$, $4 + 2$, etc.; $6 - 1$, $6 - 2$, etc.

Investigation of numbers to ten

Odds and evens to ten

Pairs

Groupings in two, three, four, i.e. 2 lots of $3 = 6$ or $2 (3) = 6$

Number sequence to sixteen, then to twenty, counting actual objects

Notation to 16, then to 20

Number line to twenty (counting on, addition and subtraction using steps along it)

Commutative and associative properties of addition. $2 + 3 = 3 + 2$ is an example of commutativity and $(2 + 3) + 4 = 2 + (3 + 4)$ an example of associativity.

'Take away' to be taught simultaneously with addition and sharing, with multiplication, so that pupils will see the relationships between them.

Odds and evens to 20

Division as sharing: how many twos in ten etc.

Two meanings are apparent here: 8 shared between 2 people; 8 shared, 2 at a time (division sign to be introduced later).

Fraction as operation; half of, a third of, etc. This gives an alternative expression to multiplication: 3 lots of 2 = 6 ⟶ a third of 6 = 2.

Investigation of composition of numbers to 16 (and then to 20), i.e. 15 + 1 = 16, 16 − 2 = 14, etc.

Most notation will be horizontal at this stage. Vertical notation may be introduced later.

Experience in expressing numbers in a variety of ways, i.e. 7 = (2 × 3) + 1 etc.

Combined operations with apparatus of numbers up to 20

Number sequence to 100

Informal introduction to two-column and three-column place-value notation in a variety of bases. Place value is the most important concept in number work.

The following addition and subtraction facts should be known (almost instant recall) before the child is allowed to progress to more formal work involving larger numbers:

1 + 1	1 + 2	1 + 3	*up to* 1 + 9
2 + 1	2 + 2	2 + 3	*up to* 2 + 9
3 + 1	3 + 2	3 + 3	*up to* 3 + 9
4 + 1	4 + 2	4 + 3	*up to* 4 + 9
5 + 1	5 + 2	5 + 3	*up to* 5 + 9
6 + 1	6 + 2	6 + 3	*up to* 6 + 9
7 + 1	7 + 2	7 + 3	*up to* 7 + 9
8 + 1	8 + 2	8 + 3	*up to* 8 + 9
9 + 1	9 + 2	9 + 3	*up to* 9 + 9

18 − 9				
17 − 9	17 − 8			
16 − 9	16 − 8	16 − 7		
15 − 9	15 − 8	15 − 7	15 − 6	
14 − 9	14 − 8	14 − 7	14 − 6	
13 − 9	13 − 8	13 − 7	13 − 6	
12 − 9	12 − 8	12 − 7	12 − 6	
11 − 9	11 − 8	11 − 7	11 − 6	etc.

10 − 9	10 − 8	10 − 7	10 − 6	*up to* 10 − 1
9 − 9	9 − 8	9 − 7	9 − 6	*up to* 9 − 1
	8 − 8	8 − 7	8 − 6	*up to* 8 − 1
		7 − 7	7 − 6	*up to* 7 − 1
				6 − 1
				5 − 1
			etc.	4 − 1
				3 − 1
			2 − 2	2 − 1
				1 − 1

A more exact knowledge of the numbers up to 100, and then beyond when the child is ready

Addition and subtraction with the numbers up to 100, and then beyond when appropriate

Horizontal and column form of notation

As preparation for multiplication, there should be counting forwards and backwards in 10, 5, 3, etc. from any starting point. (1−100 number square, number line).

Number sequence can be used for oral practice, as below:

1, 2, 3, 4, 5, etc. (Natural numbers)
1, 3, 5, 7, 9, etc. (Odd numbers)
2, 4, 6, 8, 10, etc. (Even numbers)
4, 8, 12, 16, 20, etc. (Add on 4)

Children should find as many ways as possible, within the number facts known to them, of expressing a number, for instance

$9 = 30 − 21 = 27 − 18 = (1 + 2) + 6 = 36 \div 4$ etc.

Names of fractions and a knowledge of fraction in units used in measurement

Fractional parts of whole numbers, for instance $\frac{1}{2}$ of 14

Equivalence of fractions

Simple addition and subtraction of fractions. Unit fractions

Fraction as numbers on number line

Decimal fractions — 0·1, 0·01 — from measurement

Square numbers

The shape of an odd number

The shape of an even number

The shape of a rectangular number

Prime numbers

Triangular numbers

The use of a magic square (see below) will provide stimulation as well as practice in the addition and subtraction of numbers:

8	1	6
3	5	7
4	9	2

As multiplication and division facts are discovered they should be entered in a multiplication square to be used as a ready reckoner and in other ways. All the facts up to ten times ten should be discovered practically and entered in this square and a more formal study of the multiplication tables begun. These facts must be known in all the contexts likely to be used in computation. The learning of the two, three, five, ten, four and six times tables. Whenever a table is formally studied, it should be used in every way met with in practice, within the child's experience. Thus the two times table lends itself to the study of pairs, bicycle wheels, number of hands for children and so on.

Calculators should be introduced when and where appropriate. The use of the calculator will mean that less time needs to be given to the algorithms for addition, subtraction, multiplication and division than has been the tradition in the past. It is vital that good calculator practice is developed.

The extension of multiplication facts up to 10×10.

The following basic multiplication facts should be known, *but* remember that there will be some in the class who have great problems with retention. These children will possibly never ever remember the facts and should be encouraged to use an aid to memory such as a multiplication table chart, a calculator or similar device.

1 × 1	1 × 2	1 × 3	*up to* 1 × 10
2 × 1	2 × 2	2 × 3	*up to* 2 × 10
3 × 1	3 × 2	3 × 3	*up to* 3 × 10
4 × 1	4 × 2	4 × 3	*up to* 4 × 10
5 × 1	5 × 2	5 × 3	*up to* 5 × 10
6 × 1	6 × 2	6 × 3	*up to* 6 × 10
7 × 1	7 × 2	7 × 3	*up to* 7 × 10
8 × 1	8 × 2	8 × 3	*up to* 8 × 10
9 × 1	9 × 2	9 × 3	*up to* 9 × 10
10 × 1	10 × 2	10 × 3	*up to* 10 × 10

Difficult ones to remember are:

$$6 \times 7 \quad 7 \times 6 \quad 8 \times 8 \quad 8 \times 7 \quad 7 \times 8 \quad 6 \times 8$$
$$8 \times 6 \quad 7 \times 9 \quad 9 \times 7 \quad 9 \times 9 \quad 6 \times 9 \quad 9 \times 6$$

Associative and commutative aspects of multiplication:
$a \times (b \times c) = (a \times b) \times c$ is associative, while $a \times b = b \times a$ is commutative.

Factors and multiples

Decimal fractions, operations on decimal qualities. (The most practical examples will occur with measurement of length, weight, money, area and volume.)

Relations between successive terms in the sequence and between different patterns (in other words, the difference between successive square numbers, the connection between triangle and square number).

Number patterns: square, rectangle, triangle, prime numbers

Relations between sets of numbers

Awareness of rounding off of numbers: nearest decimal place; significant figures. Significance of any measurement and discussions of accuracy and error.

Equalities and inequalities. The use of $>$ and $<$

Highest common factor and least common multiple and other related arithmetical concepts

Use of computer and other aids to computation where appropriate

Directed numbers and their relation to the number line. The addition and subtraction of directed numbers. The set of integers

Fibonacci numbers and other sequences. Connection with golden section

Fractions, equivalent fractions, inverse fractions, simple operations with fractions. Scale diagrams and simple ratio

Shape

Free play activities

Recognition of basic shapes: cuboid, cube, sphere, disc, oblong, square, circle, triangle, etc.

Sorting according to shape and size

Flat, round, straight, curved, cornered, closed, open. Some objects will roll and others will not. All work at this stage should be informal.

Next to, above, below, left, right

The comparison of two like shapes by size: larger, smaller

The continued recognition of shapes in the environment and not merely on the classroom walls

Folding, cutting, colouring

Making simple patterns. Making models from junk

Equivalence of shapes by cutting and recombining parts

Fitting together cubes and rods

Parts of shape: part—whole relationships. Folding to make halves and quarters. Patterns formed by combining shapes; mosaics, use of pegboard

Discovering of simple properties of the oblong and square and that diagonal folding can form triangles. (Do not start from the definition: a discovery of properties may take several weeks.)

Straight lines by folding and by using stretched string. Horizontal, vertical, sloping. Position on a line. (Compare number line.)

Properties of the disc and the circle; parts of a circle

Greater emphasis on correct names of shapes. (Note that the set of rectangles includes both squares and oblongs.)

Idea of symmetry can be informally introduced by paper-folding and cutting

More specific reference to 'corners'. Making of a 'square corner' by folding and fitting it into desks, books, windows, etc.

The use of a ruler in drawing straight lines

Drawing shapes from coins, tin lids etc.

Handling and recognition of cut-outs of previous shapes together with the hexagon and right-angled triangle

Making shapes (for instance, on rectangular nail board or similar apparatus) of all known shapes and discovery of other shapes by joining diagonals and by forming diamonds from mid-points of sides of square and rectangle

Hexagons and right-angled triangles introduced into pattern-making

Application of right-angle made by pupils from folded paper to discover the square corners of a rectangle, a square and a right-angled triangle

The discovery that a square can fit into the same shape, though inverted or rotated. Further experience of solid shapes, e.g. pyramids

The discovery of equal edges and other similar properties of cubes, cuboids, prisms and pyramids

An experience of shape can still be gained from constructional toys and from the construction of models in which cartons, boxes, reels, etc. are used

Making angles with Meccano strips or cardboard strips and comparison with square corners — now to be named 'right-angle'

Quadrilaterals made by strips — a comparison with the rectangle

Shape of half-circle and quarter-circle (as in clock-time recognition) by folding

Symmetry as balanced shape

Symmetry discovered in known shapes: capital letters, ink blots, leaves, fish, etc.

Folding and matching, paper tearing and cutting, to gain experience of symmetry

Area introduced as amount of surface. Measurement of area by covering with sheets of paper, stamps, cards, triangles, rectangles, squares, etc. Practice in choosing the most suitable of these units. Show that same number of units could make another shape

Discovery of shapes that will or will not fit into one another, e.g. a circular shape will not fit into a rectangle

Making models from nets: cuboid, cube, prism, cylinder

Faces and edges of these models

Classification and naming of solids. Euler's relation between numbers of vertices, edges and faces. Simple properties of different solids

Classification and naming of two-dimensional shapes. Use of Venn diagram to develop specific properties (set of squares subset of set of rectangles, various kinds of triangle, etc.) Simple properties of individual shapes and relations between shapes

Simple properties of the circle including drawing using compasses

Tessellations generally as pattern building and then related to area of regular and irregular plane shapes. Formulae for calculating the areas of rectangles, triangles and other relevant shapes. Use of tessellation for discovery of simple angle properties and other related concepts

Symmetry, bilateral and rotational (at least some groundwork) with two- and three-dimensional shapes

Angles as extent of rotation. The classification of angles as right, acute, obtuse and reflex. Angles occurring in shapes and tessellation work

Simple transformations: translation, reflection, rotation

Introduction to conic sections (parabola, hyperbola, circle, ellipse) as they occur naturally

Pythagoras's theorem with right-angled triangles

Construction of five regular polyhedra (tetrahedron, cube, octahedron, dodecahedron, icosahedron) and other solid shapes

Representation

Lay out actual objects: a favourite toy, hoops, string, etc.

Representation for each object: draw, cut out and stick

Simple relation diagrams between two sets: 'age is', 'went to', 'favourite toy is', 'likes to eat', etc. No more than six elements in set

Groundwork for block graphs: units in a straight line; the units must be equal; the units are placed very close together; the units must start from a common base line.

These stages must be covered before starting block-graph representation. It is very valuable for children to be asked to represent a given set of information in as many different forms as possible (beads suspended, matchboxes, cotton reels, Unifix, interlocking beads, milk bottles, sticky squares and circles, etc.).

Block graphs: no scale initially, as the child shoud be made to see the need for a scale. Label the scale as a continuous — and not discrete — number line.

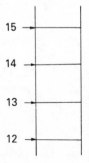

Ready-made graphs

The relation between two sets of numbers; numbers in sets; numbers on one line; numbers on two parallel lines; numbers on two intersecting lines (curve stitching); numbers within set; numbers arranged on a circle

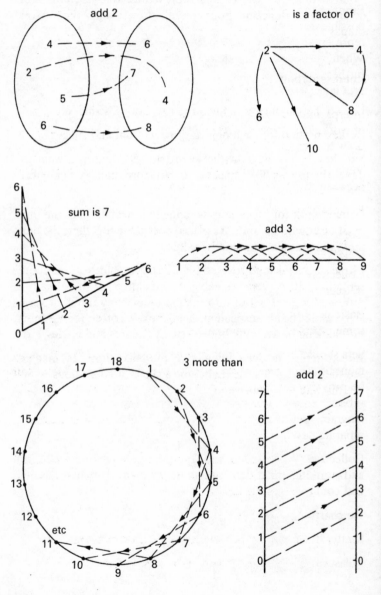

Co-ordinates: introduction via seats, battleships, pegboard bingo, patterns, maps

Relations as ordered pairs of numbers. Two sets; each element is an ordered pair on one axis.

Block graphs and alternative forms of graphical representation. Emphasis to be placed on as many different representations as possible for a single set of data rather than on one form of representation used many times with different sets of data. Whenever a graph is produced it must be used as a basis for further work and discussion. This will help the children to interpret information from a graph.

Interpretation from a graph is a sadly neglected area in this type of work, and yet in reality is more important than the ability to draw the graph.

Venn diagrams, simple relation graphs showing connection between two sets (including two sets of numbers)

Rectangular co-ordinates

Curve stitching and envelopes of curves: parabola, hyperbola, ellipse and circle (related to spatial concepts)

Collection and analysis of data including block graphs and frequency diagrams

Basic notions of chance and probability may be discussed and some practical work undertaken.

Sets should have been used as a basic language in the development of other parts of the breakdown. Ample opportunity will be provided for the development of ideas such as universal set, subset, empty set, intersection and union of sets, Venn diagrams, without these topics being represented as part of a separate development.

Collection, presentation and interpretation of both numerical and non-numerical data. Accuracy of measurements. Discrete and continuous variables

Pie charts

Scatter diagrams and pictorial interpretation of correlation

Measures of central tendency: mode, median and mean

Measurement

Measurement is taken to include length, weight, capacity (and volume), time, temperature and money as major topic areas with derived units such as area, speed and density included within the areas when appropriate. The basic units of measurement for use in the primary years are those listed below.

Basic units

The International System of metric measurement (SI) is based on a number of basic units, three of which are of concern to primary school education. These are as follows:

Quantity measure	Basic unit	Symbol	Other units	Symbol
Weight[a]	kilogram	kg	gram	g
			tonne (1000 kg)	t
Length	metre	m	kilometre	km
			centimetre	cm
			millimetre[b]	mm
Time	second	s	minute	min
			hour	h
			year	—
			month	—
			day	—

Notes:

a. 'Weight' is the layman's term for what scientists and engineers refer to as 'mass'. Scientifically, the weight of an object is the force exerted by the earth's gravitational field on the object: weight can thus be interpreted crudely as a pull towards the ground. The mass of the object is the quantity of matter the object contains. The force of attraction varies with the position of the object, but the quantity of matter remains fixed. The weight of an object can be found by using a spring balance, bathroom scale or modern direct-reading kitchen scale, but the mass has to be found by using the old-fashioned type of balance scales where an object is placed in one pan and a balance obtained by placing objects of known mass in the other.

Though this distinction between weight and mass is clear to the scientist, it is rarely made in daily life. Later on in the child's school career, when units are developed, this distinction will be relatively easy to grasp, but it is felt that in the initial stages the word 'weight' should be used in accordance with its everyday usage. The distinction between the two words can be drawn and explained at a later stage. If the teacher is concerned about this suggestion, the word 'mass' may be used when it is obviously more appropriate; however, the intention is that no undue worry should be centred around the distinction between the two words.

b. Teachers of young children may feel it is sensible to use decimetres (dm) when their pupils first start measuring length in standard units. The decimetre is a respectable submultiple of an SI unit, and it is no crime to use it. It could perhaps be dropped as the children grow older and are able to think and work confidently in centimetres.

Derived units

In general, derived units are the result of multiplications and/or divisions involving the basic units. For example, the area of a rectangular lawn 4m wide and 5m long is 4×5 square metres, written $20m^2$. The unit of area is derived from the basic units by multiplying one of them (m) by itself. If a car travels 50 metres in 5 seconds its average speed is $\frac{50}{5}$ metres per second, which can be written 10 m/s.

The unit of speed is derived from two of the basic units (m and s) by a process of division.

Here are some common derived units:

Quantity measure	Unit	Symbol	Other units	Symbol
Area	square metre	m^2	square centimetre	cm^2
Volume	cubic metre	m^3	cubic centimetre*	cm^3
Speed	metre per second	m/s	kilometre per hour	km/h
Density	kilogram per cubic metre	kg/m^3	gram per cubic centimetre	g/cm^3

*Note
This is read as 'cubic centimetre' and not 'centimetre cubed'.

Supplementary units

The following, while not strictly SI units, are nevertheless in common use.

Liquid measure. The unit name is the litre, and the symbol 'l', though the full form of the word is often used to avoid confusion with the numeral '1'. One litre is the same as one cubic decimetre, but for historical reasons the use of the litre is usually confined to fluid measurement, whereas m^3, cm^3 and so on are used for volumes in general. The millilitre (ml) is in common usage now that the standard medicine spoon measures 5 ml. $1\,\text{ml} = 1\,\text{cm}^3$

Area of land.   The hectare (ha) — which is roughly the area of two hockey pitches — is $10\,000\,\text{m}^2$.

Notational convention

The names of units and their multiples and submultiples may either be written out in full or abbreviated using the approved symbols, but no other form of abbreviation should be used. The letter 's' should not be added to a symbol to give the plural. A full stop is not written after a unit symbol unless it occurs at the end of a sentence. In the case of long numbers, figures are grouped in threes with a short space between each group. Commas should not be used, for instance 38 645 should be used instead of 38,645.

Length

Descriptive language: 'long', 'short', 'high', 'low', 'tall, 'wide', 'deep', 'narrow', etc.

Comparative language: tall, taller, tallest; wide, wider, widest etc. 'What would seem tall to a giant?' or 'Our book of tall things'.

Comparison of linear dimensions: 'longer than', 'shorter than', etc.

The ordering of lengths

The meaning of length with improvised units, experience of as many different sets of units as possible (language: 'up', 'down', 'round', 'along', 'straight', 'curved', 'sloping'). 'Fill in' the length with units: 'fill in' objects must touch. Use sets of objects such as milk straws, pencils, spills, matchboxes, etc. Find the lengths of different objects in the classroom using these sets of objects: 'so many and a bit'.

It is important to measure in several directions, not just along the horizontal plane.

The comparison of length using a single unit. This is a partially abstract situation because it obliges the children to imagine the existence of other units. Then estimate and measure.

Measurement of length using personal units, span, digit, cubit, pace, etc. (Cut a length out of card or tape and use this.)

The introduction of standard unit. Children become aware of difference in lengths of one another's units. Allow them to invent their own standard, which can be anything from a straw to a piece of structural apparatus. This can be cut up to measure a bit over; longer units can be made equivalent to, say, six standard units. This leads to an appreciation of the need for an overall standard.

Standard unit: decimetre, metre, centimetre

A familiarity with standard units: 'Bring me something longer than one metre', 'Bring me something about one metre long', etc.

The measurement of linear dimensions using rigid and flexible units ('I haven't got a curved ruler!') Things in the environment (classroom etc.). Vital statistics. This leads to computation, especially 'the difference between'.

Simple scaled length by folding string or strips of paper

Weight

The development of language in the descriptive and comparative sense: 'heavy', 'light'. The ability to lift: sorting into heavy and light sets; 'Bring me ...'

A comparison of weight: 'heavier than', 'lighter than'. Push on hand; balance

Equivalence of weight: 'weighs the same as'

Ordering of weights: visual difference and weight difference (use parcels)

Informal relationships between weight and size

Weighing with improvised units: conkers, cubes, structural apparatus, cotton reels, nails, shells, etc.

The relation between weight and volume

The introduction of standard units. Gram or kilogram? The use of weights

Measurement of weight and simple computation. Shopping lists. The weights of different parcels, two, three or four parcels, difference in weight between parcels

Weighing themselves and comparing their weights with those of other children

A comparison of same-sized boxes containing different weights

Filling identical containers with different objects and weighing them; putting them in order

Capacity

Informal treatment involving the use of a variety of materials and containers. Investigation of the nature of the properties they are playing with ('sink', 'float', 'dissolve', 'rust', 'empty', 'bubbly', 'still', etc.).

Pouring of water, sand (grain?)

(Capacity is a difficult concept, and plenty of practice will be required at this early stage.)

Filling a container by repeated pourings from a smaller container

Frequent practice with different sizes of container so that the same quantity of liquid or sand looks different in containers of different shape: 'shallow', 'deep', 'narrow', 'wide', etc.

Comparing sizes of different containers by finding out how many smaller containerfuls are needed to fill them: 'holds more than', 'holds less than', 'holds the same as'; n cups fill one bottle etc.

Graduating jar in teaspoons: bottle in cupfuls etc.

Filling of container with solid shapes: Unifix, wooden cubes, balls, etc.

The natural need for a standard unit of capacity: the litre

The use of a litre measure to find the capacities of various vessels and containers (with a practical limit of six litres)

Introduction of half-litre and smaller units as required

Millilitre introduced as the practical unit of capacity for a smaller container (standard medicine spoon holds 5 ml)

Checking of capacities of standard containers: tins, oil drums, bottles, milk churns, etc.

Collection of information about capacity

Simple addition and subtraction problems in litres

Time

Introduction to names of days, months and seasons; stories and rhymes about the seasons

'Tomorrow', 'today', 'yesterday'

Pendulum: 'faster', 'slower', (different lengths of string)

Timing by swings of a pendulum

Timing by rhythmic movement; clapping

Egg timer; metronome; candles

Clock face with hours. Association of hands of clock with regular happenings in the classroom (start of school, playtime, lunch-time, home time, etc.)

The half-hour

Clock time extended to quarter past the hour. Digital time may have to be introduced at this stage if many children have digital watches. If not, leave until later.

Primitive measures of time

Introduction to the minute

The amount of time taken to walk and run a measured distance: the distance moved in one minute etc.

Minutes in fives: folding to graduate a clock face in hours

Clock face extended to five minutes past and five minutes to the hour

Minutes after and before the next hour

Digital time

The use of 'a.m.' and 'p.m.', for their meaning only

The 24-hour clock. 24 hours = one day; 60 minutes = one hour

Timetables

Seconds pendulum; second hand. The stop-watch. 60 seconds = one minute

The use of the clock and calendar

Timing distances travelled in metres and kilometres

Shopping and money

Play shop: how much? What does it cost? (A social activity, no recording).

Make things to sell in shop and place in collection of containers: cakes, fruit, supplies for pets, etc.

Shopping with 1p coins

Recognition of coins: 1p, 2p

Shopping with 1p and 2p: change

Coin recognition: 5p, 10p (and 1p, 2p)

Shopping with 1p, 2p, 5p, 10p

Coin recognition: 20p (and 1p, 2p, 5p, 10p)

Shopping with 1p, 2p, 5p, 10p, 20p, leading to a more formal treatment of money

More difficult shopping

Coin recognition: 50p (related shape of coin of interest, and other coins)

Shopping with 50p coin

Coin recognition £1 (and other coins)

Shopping with £1 and amounts greater than £1

Bring in connected activities from length, weight and capacity and use shopping as practical vehicle for developing basic number concepts.

Many excellent games associated with shopping

Shop can become bank, post office, café, etc.

Experiment with other kinds of shop: toyshop, pet shop, etc.

Temperature

Development of language in a descriptive sense: 'hot', 'cold', 'warm'

Comparison of temperature: 'hotter than', 'colder than'

Introduction to the thermometer

Degrees Celsius and Fahrenheit

Range of temperature in environment (weather, body, boiling, freezing, etc.)

General measurement

(This is measurement based on length, weight, capacity, time, temperature and money.)

Estimate, measure and record errors in each kind of measurement

Consolidation of the concepts of weight, length, area, capacity, volume, time, temperature and money. Various instruments used in measurement of each and the correct units

Introduction of larger units when and where appropriate (kilometre, tonne)

Distinction between weight and mass and the use of the correct units. The need to calibrate instruments when measuring weight. Density as mass per unit volume

Measurement of length in straight lines and curved lines in various directions using rulers, trundle wheels, tapes and other instruments. Connections between the accuracy of the measurement and the instrument used. Scale maps and simple estimation problems using properties of the triangle and involving the measurement of angles and distances. Concept of length used together with time, to develop the idea of speed. Distance, time, speed relationships and simple graphs

Differentiation between volume and capacity and the use of the basic unit millilitre and cubic centimetre. The use of the standard units in finding the volumes and capacities of regular and irregular shapes and containers

Area introduced as amount of surface. Finding the area of regular and irregular plane shapes by filling in with unit shape and superimposing transparent grids. Connection with tessellation work. A square seen as a suitable unit for the measurement of area. The formulae for the areas of simple plane shapes. Tangram and other dissection puzzles etc. stress the conservation of area.

Concept of time extended to include the use of the 24-hour clock, the calendar and the idea of speed. Practical situations including the use of timetables, tide tables, to be explored.

Money and value should be discovered within a practical context when they arise. This should give rise to a treatment of shopping, saving and interest, fares, wages, profit and loss, etc.

Other kinds of measurement should be examined as they arise naturally.

ALGORITHMS FOR ADDITION, SUBTRACTION, MULTIPLICATION AND DIVISION

As mentioned previously, the advent of the cheap calculator is leading to a radical rethinking of the place of the traditional pencil-and-paper methods in the number work of today. In the past, a great deal of time was spent in helping the child perfect formal methods for computation despite the fact that — as the results of the APU testing show — the end product is not very encouraging. In the future we can expect calculator methods to replace many of the established practices, although at the present time it seems that many teachers either remain unconvinced of the need for a radical rejection or feel that the time for such positive action has not yet arrived. For these teachers, the following section briefly deals with recommended traditional algorithms for computation.

Computational skills and procedures

It is essential that the child fully understands the meaning of the place-value notation and has the ability to add, subtract, multiply and divide in the base of ten (that is, with ordinary numbers). Experience with bases other than ten may assist the child's understanding of the number system he or she uses in practice. Frequently children who work only in the base of ten know how to calculate but do not understand how the calculation works; they have learnt a series of rules and procedures without seeing and *understanding* the structure behind the calculations.

It can be valuable for children to experience actual representations of numbers and the place-value notation. This can be achieved with the use of such materials as Dienes multibase blocks, Tillich blocks, Unifix cubes or other equivalent sets. When multibase apparatus is used, it must be remembered that the final objective is to give the child a deeper understanding of the number system in base ten. Once a concept has been grasped with regard to the smaller bases, the concept should be developed in base ten. Some children may need to use base ten apparatus in order to reinforce the ideas developed with smaller bases; but if used in a structured way, leading to a mastery of the concepts in base ten, the actual number of smaller bases required will vary from child to child.

Addition

Initially, the calculation will involve only tens and units, but later the ideas will be extended to include hundreds and thousands. It is useful to express numbers as a sum of thousands, hundreds, tens and units to stress the meaning of each digit within the number, for example:

$$6342 \longrightarrow (6000 + 300 + 40 + 2)$$

When a number is expressed as such a sum, it is better to enclose the sum within brackets to emphasise that this is a decomposition of the number into its component parts. This form of expression may be used by the teacher in the initial stages of the recording of calculations.

Addition rarely presents children with a great deal of difficulty. The notation used in the recording tends to follow the logical sequence of steps encountered with the use of apparatus. Two stages are indicated in the development of notation: introductory notation stressing the operation; notation for the mental operation. The first stage can be a lengthy process and should not be overdone. However, it is a link between the physically performed operation with apparatus and the notation suitable for quick calculation. It is better to keep this as a blackboard method for use by the teacher.

(1)

$$\begin{array}{r} 24 \quad (20+4) \\ +\underline{67} \rightarrow (60+7) \\ \hline (80+11) \rightarrow (80+10+1) \rightarrow (90+1) \rightarrow 91 \end{array}$$

(2)

$$\begin{array}{r} 24 \\ +67 \\ \hline 91 \end{array}$$

In (1), the 10 from the sum of 4 and 7 causes no difficulty.

As a rule, children are rushed into the use of mental operation with accompanying jargon concerning the use of the 'carrying figure'. The significance of the 10 is clear with this notation. In (2), the complete 10 from the sum of the units is sometimes recorded above the line or below the space for the answer.

Subtraction

The method of subtraction which follows directly from the use of apparatus of any kind is that of decomposition. This is a method young children will understand. The stages outlined in the development are those described previously.

(1)

$$\begin{array}{r} 45 \quad (40+5) \quad (30+15) \\ -\underline{29} \longrightarrow (20+9) \longrightarrow (20+9) \\ \hline (10+6) \longrightarrow 16 \end{array}$$

One of the tens has needed to be decomposed into 10 units.

(2)

$$\begin{array}{r} 45 \\ -29 \\ \hline 16 \end{array}$$

Alternatively, a light crossing-out may be used:

(2)
$$\begin{array}{r} ^3\cancel{4}5^{10} \\ -29 \\ \hline 16 \end{array}$$

or

$$\begin{array}{r} ^3\cancel{4}5^{1} \\ -29 \\ \hline 16 \end{array}$$

There are three other methods of subtraction of which the teacher should be aware. These are outlined below.

Complementary addition method. This is essentially an extension of the ideas of 'more than' introduced at an earlier stage. It involves finding what number must be added to the smaller number to make the larger one.

$$7 - 3 = \boxed{} \longrightarrow 3 + \boxed{} = 7$$

'What do I need to add to 3 to make 7?'

$$84 - 37 \longrightarrow 37 \relbar 40 \relbar 80 \relbar 84$$

$$+3 \quad +40 \quad +4$$

$$\underbrace{}_{47}$$

As a formal method of subtraction this has obvious short-comings, especially if the difference between the numbers is considerable.

Simple equal addition. This method involves 'rounding up' the smaller number to make the subtraction easier. For example:

$$\begin{array}{ccc} 85 & (85+2) & 87 \\ -38 \longrightarrow & (38+2) \longrightarrow & -40 \\ \hline & & \overline{47} \end{array}$$

39

The 38 is rounded up to 40 by the addition of 2. The difference (85−38) then becomes (87−40), which causes little difficulty.

The concept upon which this method is based, $a - b = (a + c) - (b + c)$, is a difficult one for children to understand. This method of subtraction is not one that is suitable for young children. However, it can be used at a later stage provided the pupils have had a considerable amount of practice in the above concept (coloured rods are especially suitable). The process is most suitable for pairs of numbers less than 100 as there are obvious difficulties with rounding up if the numbers are large.

Conventional equal addition. This method involves the systematic addition of 10, 100, 1000 and so on to both numbers in order to make the subtraction easier. For example:

$$
\begin{array}{cccc}
53 & (50+3) & (50+3+(10\times 1)) & (50+13) \\
-29 & (20+9) & (20+9+(1\times 10)) & (30+\ 9) \\
& & & (20+\ 4) \longrightarrow 24
\end{array}
$$

Ten is added to both numbers. In the case of the larger number the 10 is thought of as 'ten units', and with the smaller number the 10 is thought of as 'one 10'. This method is again based on the concept $a - b = (a + c) - (b + c)$, and is difficult for young children to understand.

If this method is used in the classroom it is important that expressions like 'borrowing and paying back' are not used. The development of the notation should be along the lines outlined previously.

$$
\begin{array}{ccc}
62 & (60+2) & (60+12) \\
-34 & (30+4) & (40+\ 4) \\
& & (20+\ 8) \quad / \quad 28
\end{array}
$$

Summary of subtraction ideas. Four methods have been discussed. The complementary addition method occurs as an extension of the early notions encountered by the child. The simple equal addition method is useful as a mental process when the numbers are small (ideally tens and units only) but has shortcomings when they are large. The other two methods are rivals for the claim to be the formal method of subtraction to be adopted by a school. Brighter children may benefit from a knowledge of both methods, but with pupils of average and below average ability the introduction of two formal methods of subtraction will lead to confusion. A decision has then to be taken about which of the two methods to use.

Decomposition is the method which follows directly and logically from the use of apparatus and is easy for children to understand. The main criticism of the method is that when the stage has been reached for calculations to be done quickly the equal addition method is better; but if decomposition is taught effectively and ample practice is allowed, the calculation will be just as quick. In fact, at this stage, the two processes involved in the calculation, regrouping and subtracting, can be separated and done one at a time by the decomposition method. By the equal addition method the process of regrouping and subtracting tends to be mixed throughout the calculation.

$$
\begin{array}{ccc}
 & 2\ \ 17\ \ 5\ \ 12 & \qquad 2\ \ 17\ \ 5\ \ 12 \\
3\ 7\ 6\ 2 \quad \text{regroup} \quad 3\ 7\ 6\ 2 \quad \text{subtract} \quad 3\ 7\ 6\ 2 \\
\ \ 8\ 3\ 4 \qquad\qquad\quad\ \ 8\ 3\ 4 \qquad\qquad\quad\ \ 8\ 3\ 4 \\
\hline
 & & 2\ \ 9\ 2\ 8
\end{array}
$$

It is recommended that decomposition be adopted if a formal method is required.

Multiplication

(1)
$$
\begin{array}{rl}
63 & (60+3) \\
\times\ 7 \longrightarrow & 7 \\
& 21 \quad\text{——}\quad 3\times 7 \\
& 420 \quad\text{——}\quad 60\times 7 \\
\hline
& 441
\end{array}
$$

(2)
$$
\begin{array}{r}
63 \\
\times\ 7 \\
\hline
441
\end{array}
$$

A knowledge of the basic multiplication facts from 1×1 to 10×10 is of paramount importance.

Long multiplication is not recommended for children at primary school.

Division

The two aspects of division must be stressed if a formal approach to division is to be understood. These are the aspects of, firstly, sharing and, secondly, of 'How many lots of?' The examples indicate the stages in each process and the development of the notation.

Sharing

(1)

$$5 \overline{)\ 62}$$

$$10 + 2 \longrightarrow 12$$
$$5 \overline{)\ 60 + 2}$$
$$\begin{array}{r} 50 \\ \hline 10 \end{array} \rceil \begin{array}{l} \rightarrow 10 \\ 12 \\ \underline{10} \\ 2 \end{array}$$

(2)

$$\begin{array}{r} 12 \\ 5 \overline{)\ 62} \\ \underline{5} \\ 12 \\ \underline{10} \\ 2 \end{array}$$

The six complete tens are shared between the five, giving each one ten (shown above the line) and leaving one ten remainder. This one ten is decomposed into ten units and added to the two units, making twelve units which are then shared between the five, giving each two (shown above the line) and leaving a remainder of two.

How many lots of?

(1) $65 \div 12$

The lots of twelve can be formed by the successive subtractions of twelve from 65 until the number remaining is less than twelve.

$$\begin{array}{l} 65 - \\ \underline{12} \qquad \text{once} \end{array}$$

$$53 -$$
$$12 \quad \text{twice}$$

$$41 -$$
$$12 \quad \text{3 times} \qquad \text{thus } 65 = (5 \times 12) + 5$$

$$29 -$$
$$12 \quad \text{4 times}$$

$$17 -$$
$$12 \quad \text{5 times}$$
$$5$$

(2)
$$
\begin{array}{r}
5 \\
12 \overline{\smash{)}65} \\
60 \\
\hline
5
\end{array}
$$

$$1 \times 12 = 12$$
$$2 \times 12 = 24$$
$$3 \times 12 = 36$$
$$4 \times 12 = 48$$
$$5 \times 12 = 60$$
$$6 \times 12 = 72$$

The reverse of (1) by building up lots of twelve.

FURTHER READING

The following teachers' books are valuable in advising about methodology relating to the mathematical development outlined in this section.

Schools Council, *Early Mathematical Experiences (Water. Raw Materials; Towards Number. Apparatus, Toys and Games; Passage of Time. Rhymes and Stories; Home corner. The Family; Outdoor Activities. The Environment; Space and Shape. Comparisons)* (Addison-Wesley).

R. Hollands, *Ginn Mathematics* (Ginn).

B. Frobisher and I. Gloyn, *Infant Mathematics* (Ward Lock).

D. Lumb and A. Papendick, *Mathematics 5 to 9* (Murray).

Nuffield, British Council, *Mathematics: The First 3 Years* (Chambers).

H. Fletcher *et al.*, *Mathematics for Schools* (2nd edition) (Addison-Wesley).

E. Albany (ed.) *et al.*, *Nuffield Maths 5–11* (Longman).

D. and M.M. Lumb, *Number Rhymes*: First collection and Second collection (Learning Materials).

A. Thomas and M. Bannister *Number Work for Infants* (Blackwell).

A. Brighouse *et al.*, *Peak Mathematics* (Nelson).

K. Auckland *et al.*, *Primary Mathematics* (Globe).

A. MacCallum *et al.*, *SPMG Mathematics* (Heinemann).

5

The Mathematically More Able Child

During the last few years a great deal of attention has been drawn to the needs of gifted children. Unfortunately there is some confusion about the actual definition of 'giftedness', and no clear consensus of opinion seems to exist on the subject. Sometimes the gifted child is, somewhat clinically, taken as being one belonging to the top 2 per cent of the ability range. This poses the question of how to measure the ability of the child and which range of ability to take: should it be the class, the year group within the school, the year group within the local authority? To avoid a lengthy discussion of the definition it is proposed to define the group of primary school children who are the subject of this section as those who exhibit a markedly superior development of performance and achievement in mathematics and who have done so reasonably consistently from their earlier years. For the sake of brevity these children will be referred to as 'mathematically more able'.

IDENTIFYING THE MATHEMATICALLY MORE ABLE CHILD

Some pupils stand out in the classroom as being more able in mathematics, but many teachers are concerned that their own lack of confidence in the subject can sometimes obscure this estimation of children's mathematical ability. Then the child who is markedly more able in this area may simply be identified as a good performer in the classroom and the special mathematical potential never given a chance to develop. This can be avoided by considering some pointers to mathematical 'more ableness' which will be apparent in the day-to-day contact in the classroom.

Classroom pointers

The mathematically more able child is likely to:

Be able to memorise quickly

Be able to work independently

Learn easily and readily.

Show an ability to handle numbers, though this may be simply an ability to compute. There are many mathematicians who will admit to being no good at arithmetic. Schools using arithmetic tests to measure mathematical performance need to take note.

Follow complex directions and instructions easily.

Show an overall ability in other subject areas. Though there are many children who fall into this category, there are others who show an outstanding ability in mathematics but are average in other subjects.

Show a great deal of curiosity about the world around him or her and be particularly interested in cause and effect.

Show a marked superiority in problem-solving activities.

Have good hand-eye motor co-ordination, though sometimes the handwriting of such children lags way behind their reading and other skills. In activities requiring a lot of meaningless copying they easily become bored.

Exhibit keen powers of observation, discriminating between important and unimportant details.

Show great powers of reasoning, of dealing with abstractions, of generalising from specific facts, of understanding meanings and seeing relationships.

Show alertness and a quick response to new ideas.

Display a superiority in the quantity and quality of his or her vocabulary, with fluent speech. (There will sometimes be a reluctance to write things down.)

Be able to work for long periods with persistence and total absorption.

Be compulsively perfectionist about his or her own achievements and impatient with second best.

Be able to listen to only part of the teacher's explanation, and then withdraw into private thoughts — of thinking on ahead.

Show great pleasure in jigsaws and constructional toys.

Use very sophisticated criteria for sorting and classification.

Have an ability to argue, question, reason, etc. Such a child often uses arguments based on 'if', 'then', 'either', 'because', etc.

Have a tendency to miss out the intermediate steps in a logical argument.

Reverse a train of thought if necessary.

Strive for an elegant solution where possible.

Have a dislike of writing out answers to problems which can be solved mentally.

Have an ease of grasping the essence of a problem.

Display great precision in practical work.

Be able to perceive and organise mathematical information, grasping the formal structure of a problem.

Be able to retain methods of solving and principles of approach.

Have a great liking for the subject.

Display an ability to process information with clear thinking and economy of solution.

Show an easy use of symbols.

Have an open-mindedness, with the result that evidence will be considered and the point of view changed according to the evidence.

Show economy of thought and compression of arguments.

Be able to see pattern in number, and to use that pattern on future occasions.

It is worth noting that mathematical ability frequently shows itself at a very early age and tends to persist, and that there are some very shy, reserved and unassertive children who are very able in the subject.

There are obvious dangers in producing a list of so many characteristics, and it is not claimed that every child who is mathematically more able will be identified by every single item; it is more that a cluster of characteristics tends to apply.

Standardised tests

A more objective approach is to use a standardised test as a screening device for a preliminary identification of the more able child. When choosing a test it is important to select one that tests mathematical attainment rather than arithmetical competence and relational rather than instrumental understanding.

Extreme caution must be taken in interpreting the score obtained. The test manual must be consulted for a meaningful interpretation of the result. If several tests are used, then a good performance on any one occasion should be interpreted as an indication of mathematical potential even if the performances on the other occasions were merely adequate. Latent mathematical ability must be located and developed if the primary teacher is to be able to claim that each child has been developed to his or her full potential. (For a more detailed discussion of tests see Chapter 12.)

WHAT TO DO WITH THE MORE ABLE CHILD

Having identified a child as mathematically more able, the next question is what to do with that child. The Cockcroft Report is quite clear in demanding that specific provision should be made in the primary school for mathematically more able children. It is not sufficient for such children to be left to work through a textbook or set of cards. They should not be given repetitive practice of processes they have already mastered. As mentioned in Chapter 1, Her Majesty's Inspectors encountered a repetitive practice of process in one-third of the classes they visited during their survey of primary schools. It is easy to forget the needs of the more able child in the hustle and bustle of the classroom, especially as such a child is not as dependent on the teacher as the less able child at the other end of the ability range.

Suitable strategies for meeting the various needs of the more able child can be illustrated by reference to the following teacher self-appraisal guide.

Self-appraisal guide for the teacher

(1) Do you leave the child who is more able in mathematics to work through the textbooks or sets of work-cards, usually in isolation and with only occasional contact?

(2) Do you combine more rapid progress through the syllabus with more demanding work related to topics already encountered — as suggested in Cockcroft?

(3) Are more able children given opportunities to undertake activities and investigations which encourage the development of generalisation and abstraction?

(4) Do such children have ready access to library and other resource materials, both inside and outside the school? Are books and other materials available within the classroom which will enable the more able child to explore in depth and go beyond the normal mathematical curriculum?

(5) As a teacher do you:

Dominate the classroom, or allow the more able children to select and pursue some topics of their own choice?

Use open-ended questions, with an emphasis on generalisation, analysis and synthesis — or do you ask closed questions with an emphasis on specific facts and rote memory?

Utilise the interests and abilities of the more able children when planning projects and general work?

Promote discussion and debate?

Allow for investigation, problem-solving and practical work?

(6) Are there children in your classes who continually score full marks? Children who always get all their sums right are probably not being stretched.

How well did you perform in the appraisal? When this guide has been used with groups of teachers, the answer has usually been 'Not very well.'

What should we teach?

If it is clearly not sufficient for more able pupils to be left to work through a textbook on their own, and if they must be given opportunities to undertake activities that help to develop their powers of generalisation and abstraction, there arises the inevitable question of content. Fortunately, the DES publication *Mathematics 5–11*[1] provides us with the following list of extension topics for children up to the age of eleven:

(1) Calculations involving the four operations, using numbers with up to two decimal places, and the addition and subtraction of vulgar fractions.

(2) Further measures, including speed, force, pressure and density.

(3) Simple ideas of probability.

(4) A simple approach to topological notions, (ideas of connectedness, as explained in a number of mathematical topic books for children).

(5) An extended appreciation of broader aspects of number such as modular arithmetic, index notation and standard form, number sequences, number games and puzzles.

(6) Symbols of algebra for stating logical patterns, following abstraction and generalisation in arithmetic.

(7) Practical enquiry into relationships between measures of different shapes: volume of cone/volume of cylinder, area of rectangles and parallelograms on same base with equal heights.

(8) Practical experience involving further kinds of measuring apparatus: height-finding using clinometer; simple theodolite work; simple pendulums of varying lengths.

(9) Experience with refined measuring instruments as appropriate: micrometer, feeler gauge and fine balances.

(10) Practical situations involving experience of compound measures, as appropriate: speed, density, pressure, consumption (miles per gallon) etc.

(11) Easy calculations with compound measures, as appropriate.

(12) Symmetry of two- and three-dimensional shapes. Making symmetrical shapes on squared paper and isometric paper; using mirrors, consideration of reflections of shapes; constructing of images on squared, isometric and plain paper using this property; consideration and discussion of the simple symmetry of three-dimensional objects.

(13) Angles: the use of the protractor.

Measures in degrees of fixed angles.

The angle as a measure of turn: turning about a fixed point: whole turn; half turn, extending to the physical world;

movement in PE, locomotive engines, levers, pulleys, swing bridges, cranes, rotation in mechanics.

Rotation measurement in degrees.

Measurement of angles: hands of the clock, work with the compass including three-figured bearings (036°, 168°) and compass bearings (N48°W). Angles between lines and the formal naming of an angle: angle ABE = 75°.

(14) Rotational symmetry. Introduction to and investigations of shapes possessing rotational symmetry. Making patterns based on rotation using congruent shapes. Practical work on the determination of the order of rotational symmetry.

(15) Pie charts. These circular charts are sometimes used to represent information where there are not too many variables.

(16) Scatter graphs. These are graphs in which two pieces of information (two variables or statistics) about each member of a set are represented simultaneously. This type of graph involves the first notions of correlation. Scatter graphs reveal relationships that might easily pass unnoticed or — which is equally important — show that a relationship does not exist when the scatter is random. A simple example of a scatter graph could be drawn by the plotting of height against reach for each child in the class. This might reveal a scatter of points which has an approximate linear relationship.

It must be stressed that these further skills and concepts are ones which *teachers with the appropriate knowledge* might consider *appropriate for some children*. This list provides a suitable starting-point for teachers wishing to identify topics where it is possible to develop sideways as well as forwards.

In this way it is possible to provide activities which stretch the child with familiar ideas instead of always moving on to new topics. The main emphasis is on *extension*.

REFERENCES

1. DES, *Mathematics 5–11*: A handbook of suggestions by HM Inspectors (HMSO, 1979).

FURTHER READING

L. Burton, *The Teaching of Mathematics to Young Children Using a Problem-Solving Approach, Educational Studies in Mathematics, 11* (1980).

L. Burton, *Thinking Things Through, Problem-Solving in Mathematics* (Blackwell, 1984).

A. Straker, *Mathematics for Gifted Children*, project report (Longman, 1982). Contains many suggestions for materials and ideas for the classroom.

A. Wood, *Making Changes — Mathematics Curriculum, Enrichment Packs for Gifted Children —* a wealth of material (Globe, 1982).

6

Children with Learning Difficulties in Mathematics

WHICH CHILDREN?

The focus of attention here is that group of children who experience difficulty in the learning of mathematics in the primary years. There have been a number of estimates of the number of children with learning difficulties: the Warnock Committee[1] talked about one child in every five, Brennan identified $12\frac{1}{2}$ per cent in the Schools Council Project *Curriculum Needs of Slower Learning Pupils*,[2] and the DES Primary Report[3] showed the results of a mathematics test where between 10 and 15 per cent of children had difficulty in counting and adding accurately when using groups of tens and units. For the purposes of this discussion the proportion of children will be taken as approximately the bottom 20 per cent of the ability range in mathematics at any one time. Many children will experience difficulty with the subject at some time during their school career, but this does not mean they will always have difficulty with it.

The problems of the child with learning difficulties in mathematics appear to be many and varied, and possible solutions are far from easy to find. Some of the problems affect parts of the school curriculum other than mathematics, but there are some factors which appear to be almost unique to mathematics.

Many children identified as belonging to the bottom 20 per cent of the ability range in mathematics have developed a sense of failure and frustration in the primary years, and many teachers show similar signs of anger, failure and frustration when trying to cope with the problem of teaching the subject to this group. 'Do you know any suitable materials?' is a question often asked where the word 'suitable' not only means at an appropriate mathematical level but also written in simple, direct language.

When simple arithmetic was the staple diet of the primary school, the level of language comprehension did not necessarily have any great effect on the mathematics. Now with the advent of non-arithmetical topics and methods of learning based on investigation, discovery, problem-solving and questioning, the lack of linguistic skill can be one more reason for failure.

THE CAUSES OF LEARNING DIFFICULTIES

Let us now examine some of the possible causes of learning difficulties in mathematics. There appear to be two basic kinds of cause of learning difficulty: external factors, which are not directly related to the content of the subject; and internal factors, which are very much related to the content. These will now be discussed in turn.

External causes

Three main clusters of external factors can be identified: medical, social and emotional; absence from school; and language.

Medical, social and emotional causes

If a child is handicapped by some physical disability, then he or she may be denied the opportunity to build up knowledge of things in the environment through the use of bodily movements involving different senses. For example, if a child is for some reason prevented from moving various household objects and toys he or she may not experience the activities of pushing and pulling. This may affect the acquisition of basic concepts in measurement.

Children with hearing problems are denied access to the expressive speech and language which is essential for the effective communication of experiences and ideas. Similarly, those with restricted vision are denied those aspects of learning acquired by imitating other children in the class.

Many children are very anxious with regard to mathematics. Excessive anxiety can lead to blushing, sweaty palms, fidgeting or becoming easily upset in class, and it has been noticed that anxious children often increase their level of anxiety as they get older. Sometimes anxiety is the cause of learning problems in mathematics and sometimes the learning problem is the cause of anxiety. It is also apparent that some children who have difficulty in sorting out their own personal problems are unable to solve mathematical problems. Other children with emotional problems have very poor powers of concentration; the span of concentration is short and the intensity weak.

The root cause of learning difficulty for some children is their limited memory skill. Mathematics is a subject where things do have to be memorised and recalled for future use.

Some children with learning difficulties find it hard to conform to the organisational structure within the classroom. They are unable to work in a group along with other children. They are rude, speak out of turn, disrupt any kind of order, are easily distracted, either influence or are ready to be influenced by others, and so on. Other children have attention problems, allowing themselves to be distracted; they rarely listen and their thoughts frequently wander. Other social characteristics to look out for are: a lack of ability to finish an assignment even if supervised; a lack of self-confidence, initiative and responsibility, a lack of ability to relate well to other children in the class; a low tolerance level for change; a lack of ability to follow instructions and to organise tasks which in turn result in an almost total dependence upon the teacher in terms of learning style.

Absence from school

Mathematics is a sequential subject, and a child's ability to master a skill or grasp a concept is dependent upon his or her mastery or grasp of subordinate skills or concepts. Obviously, a child who is absent from school a great deal will be missing key lessons which will affect his or her basic understanding of a subject. Children who are absent for a continuous period of time are usually missed and the teacher is thus able to take appropriate steps which will allow them to catch up on the missing work on their return. Those who are absent for short periods, however, can present problems if a key lesson has been missed and the teacher is not aware of the fact.

Language

Of all the problems connected with learning difficulties in mathematics those related to language seem to be mentioned the most by teachers in the classroom. The extent of the problem can be illustrated when it is realised that a child of eight may have to be familiar with the following list of 350 special words related to mathematics in addition to the normal vocabulary assumed to have been acquired by children of that age. The list was produced by a group of experienced primary teachers in the north-east of England engaged on a local curriculum project, and is based on those words teachers expected the children to know and those found to be used by authors in a sample of commercially available mathematics schemes.

The extent of the problem can be illustrated with reference to a typical class of 28 eight- to nine-year-olds in which four children were found to 'know' at a verbal level fewer than 90 of the following words:

week	fifty	high/higher/highest/height
month	sixty	low/lower/lowest
year	seventy	thick/thicker/thickest/thickness
yesterday	eighty	thin/thinner/thinnest
today	ninety	wide/wider/widest/width
tomorrow	hundred	narrow/narrower/narrowest
hour	red	broad/broader/broadest/breadth
minute	black	heavy/heavier/heaviest
o'clock	blue	light/lighter/lightest
past	white	dark/darker/darkest
morning	yellow	big/bigger/biggest
afternoon	orange	large/larger/largest
Sunday	green	small/smaller/smallest
Monday	brown	little/littler/littlest
Tuesday	(maroon)	tall/taller/tallest
Wednesday	pink	short/shorter/shortest
Thursday	first	long/longer/longest/length
Friday	second	deep/deeper/deepest/depth
Saturday	third	hard/harder/hardest
January	fourth	soft/softer/softest
February	last	far/farther/farthest
March	digit	near/nearer/nearest
April	cubit	soon/sooner/soonest
May	span	late/later/latest
June	pace	more/most
July	stride	less/least
August	foot	greater/greatest

55

September	measure	few/fewer/fewest
October	pour	fill/full/fuller/fullest
November	arrow	empty/emptier/emptiest
December	sign	upright/level
Spring	count	up/down
Summer	sequence	under/over
Autumn	increase	left/right
Winter	decrease	odd/even
zero/nothing/	shape	before/after
nought	solid	below/above
one	cube	equal/unequal
two	cone	vertical/horizontal
three	cuboid	inside/outside
four	cylinder	behind/in front of
five	sphere	underneath/on top of
six	prism	tessellate/tessellation
seven	tetrahedron	symmetry/symmetrical
eight	plane	reflect/reflection
nine	square	rotate/rotation
ten	triangle	translate/translation
eleven	rectangle	slope/sloping
twelve	oblong	parallelogram
thirteen	circle	trapezium
fourteen	diamond	diagonal
fifteen	oval	circumference
sixteen	ellipse	perimeter
seventeen	polygon	line
eighteen	pentagon	edge
nineteen	hexagon	corner
twenty	octagon	vertex/vertices
thirty	quadrilateral	face
forty	rhombus	surface
right angle	round	add/addition
equilateral	spiky	subtract/subtraction
blunt	tough	multiply/multiplication
hollow	across	divide/division
almost	crooked	partition/partitioning
nearly	pointed	map/mapping
between	match	difference
next to	equivalent	take away
every	sort	remainder
the same as	equal/unequal	share

many	quarter	capacity
makes	times	mass
estimate	exact/exactly	weight
tally	shop/shopping	gram
unit/long/flat/block	sell/sold	kilogram
bead	buy/bought	metre
counter	spend	centimetre
brick	change	litre
peg	penny	millilitre
pattern	pence	balance
together	pound	day
double	coin	season
half	area	pyramid
third	volume	

The reader may like to speculate on the group of words found to cause the greatest difficulty in the classroom. Invariably this turns out to be the positional words such as 'next to', 'underneath', 'on top of', 'behind' and so on, not the technical terms used in mathematics as might be expected. Details of this work can be found in the handbook of the *Early Mathematics Diagnostic Kit*[4] produced by the author.

Obviously an assessment of the learning problems related to language involves more than simply a count of the number of words a child is able to understand and use. Many words have a number of different meanings and nuances, as the following examples of alternative meanings produced by a group of eight-year-olds illustrates:

unit: 'where you put books and things'

tough: 'when you are a good fighter'

cuboid: 'what you play snooker with'

sphere: 'when you are scared of something'

prism: 'where you keep bad men'

symmetry: 'a graveyard'

surface: 'bottom of the seas'

member: 'when you go into a bar for a drink you have to be a member'

metre: 'a square thing you put money in'

plane: 'a picture of an aeroplane'

ellipse: 'a picture of a pair of lips'

Readers may like to speculate on the cause of the mix-up in meaning.

Many children develop an incomplete understanding of the meaning of a word as a result of some of the medical problems referred to earlier. Some words are particularly difficult to illustrate. For example, you can teach the word 'cone', but it is difficult to say 'This is a less.'

Language problems are not only confined to vocabulary. When the child starts to record his work in school, symbols other than words are used. In addition to the ten basic numerals 0, 1, 2, 3, 4, 5, 6, 7, 8, 9, there are a range of other symbols such as $+, -, =, \rightarrow, ( )$ and so on. The way these symbols are used can lead to many problems as the following two examples illustrate.

John. John had just about mastered left-to-right orientation in his reading. He was fine when symbols were used in his number work as a direct replacement for words in a sentence, as with

three   add   two   makes   five
3   +   2   =   5

but completely floored by the notation

$$(3,2) \xrightarrow{\text{add}} 5$$

which requires him to scan the whole line for meaning.

Sue. Sue had struggled for a long time with the numerals 0, 1, 2, 3, 4, 5, 6, 7, 8, 9 in relation to the number of objects in a collection. Unfortunately, just as she had gained confidence the same numerals were used by the teacher to stand for two digit numbers.

The last example illustrates the difficulties caused by mathematics by using combinations of symbols to stand for something else with the position of the individual symbol having significance. By the age of eight, the child may have seen the symbols used in the following ways:

1	2	12	21	(1,2)
(2,1)	2(1)	1(2)	1·2	2·1
1·2	2·1	$\frac{1}{2}$	$\frac{2}{1}$	$\frac{1}{2}$

$^2/_1$ $1 + 2$ $2 + 1$ $2 - 1$ 2×1

1×2 $2 \div 1$ $1 \div 2$ etc.

Later the size of each symbol is changed as well as the position to produce additional mathematical meanings, for example:

2^3 3^2 2_3

Generally, it is felt that many children may be rushed into the use of excessive symbolism far too early.

The relation between clusters

A Venn diagram (see below) seems to be a suitable way of illustrating these factors as they exist for many children in the classroom:

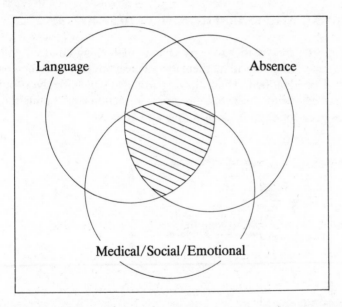

Although extreme cases of any of these external factors will lead to the problems being so great as to be beyond the capacity of the class teacher to resolve, there are many children in ordinary classes whose learning difficulties are caused by some combinations of these factors. Given the day-to-day crises of school life, which affect both staff and pupils, any attempt to unravel these causes can be very difficult. Many children are in the shaded area, their problems being a combination of factors from each group.

Internal causes

Other learning difficulties can often be traced to a lack of understanding of some aspect or aspects of the school's mathematics curriculum. This may be a skill, a technique, a concept or a practice. Frequently children between the ages of seven and thirteen are expected to build their learning upon a very shaky foundation of early mathematical concepts. It is essential that all children should develop a very solid understanding of *colour*, *shape* and *size* before being expected to progress to more advanced work. Pupils' learning problems can often be traced to a lack of understanding of one of these key concepts.

COPING WITH LEARNING DIFFICULTIES

If the teacher is to have any chance of helping children with learning difficulties in mathematics, a clear strategy of campaign must be identified. The following strategy, which involves four clear stages of diagnosis, prescription, action and evaluation, has been found to be both simple and effective:

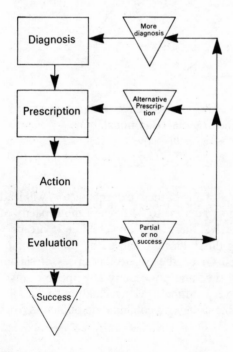

Diagnosis

The teacher must be in a position to identify the learning problems the child is experiencing. This can be done in one, or more, of the following ways: through day-to-day contact with the child, class work, discussion and external tests.

Day-to-day contact with the child

The class teacher who is in daily contact with a particular child will be aware of some of the difficulties that the child is having. Such information, though it tends to be subjective, is very valuable. Inevitably, teachers with large classes will find it more difficult to amass detailed information than those whose classes are smaller.

Class work

As the child gets older, he or she will be required to do more written work in class. Such work can give an indication of some learning difficulties, but unfortunately it is not possible to be at the side of the child every time some form of recording is undertaken.

Discussion

Regular discussion with the child about his or her work can reveal many learning problems. Dialogue of this kind must be encouraged with all pupils.

External tests

A formalised test can give an objective indication of the strengths and weaknesses of the child's mathematical ability. Unfortunately most commercially available tests only give a single score, or mathematical age, without diagnosing the actual learning problems.

The author has found the Nelson *Profile* test[4] to be particularly useful with older primary school children and has produced the *Early Mathematics Diagnostic Kit*[5] for use with younger children.

Prescription

On the basis of the diagnosis, the teacher should be able to prescribe a particular course of action. To be in a position to prescribe a programme for the child the teacher must be aware of a wide range of suitable resources. These resources will include apparatus, books, worksheets, workbooks, computer programs and so on as well as suggested activities and other strategies.

It is not possible here to review the range of commercially produced textbook schemes with regard to their suitability for the less able child in the four-to-eleven age range as the majority have only been found useful in part. The reading age assumed by many authors is far in excess of that actually achieved by the children. However, parts of some commercial schemes have been found useful in certain topic areas.

References to suitable material, together with advice about different strategies, is included in the *Early Mathematics Diagnostic Kit.*

Action

There is no magical way of organising how any suggested programme of work is implemented. Certainly a great deal of patience is needed for the effective teaching of the child with learning difficulties. The following suggestions may be useful.

(1) When planning work, Keep It Simple and Sensible: remember the KISS principle.

(2) Do not rush into introducing symbols and signs too early. The child must understand the quantities and processes for which they stand.

(3) Always endeavour to achieve an understanding of what has been learnt. A suitable progression is: Do — Understand — Practise — Consolidate — Memorise. Memorisation is difficult for many children.

(4) Frequent revision is essential because of the child's poor powers of retention.

(5) Initial concepts of number must come from real things in the child's environment

(6) Readiness is vital for effective learning. Every effort must be made to prepare the child for the next stage by integrating and consolidating previous learning to a level which anticipates the new.

(7) Quality of learning is more important than quantity.

(8) When apparatus is used, care must be taken that the

interest of the child does not become too centred on the operation of the apparatus rather than on the mathematical concept or principle involved.

(9) Use language the child can understand. Many children with learning difficulties use restricted colloquial language. The important thing is to communicate with the child. More precise mathematical language can be developed later.

(10) Do not assume an independence in learning in the child. Most children with learning difficulties are very dependent upon the teacher.

(11) If additional help is available in the classroom, take care that responsibility for the child is not transferred, either consciously or subconsciously, to the other person. This can easily happen where there is a remedial withdrawal system in school.

(12) Try, above all else, to develop in the child a positive attitude towards mathematics as an interesting and attractive subject in which he or she can gain success and pleasure.

Evaluation

Evaluation is an integral part of the process but is often neglected by teachers. In some respect the four strategies for diagnosis can be applied to evaluation: day-to-day contact, class work, discussion and external tests. It is useful to monitor the child's progress for some months afterwards to ensure satisfactory progress even if the learning difficulties have been resolved. A suitable list of key concepts, skills and practices against which a child's progress can be checked is given in the later section on evaluation (see Chapter 12).

REFERENCES

1. M. Warnock, *Special Educational Needs* (HMSO, 1978).

2. W.K. Brennan, *Curricular Needs of Slow Learning Pupils*, Schools Council Working Paper 63 (Evans–Methuen, 1978).

3. DES, *Primary Education in England,* A survey by HM Inspectors of Schools (HMSO, 1987).

4. N. France, *Profile of Mathematical Skills* (NFER-Nelson, 1979).

5. D. and M.M. Lumb, *Early Mathematics Diagnostic Kit* (NFER-Nelson, 1987).

FURTHER READING

E. Biggs, *Teaching Mathematics, 7–13, Slow Learning and More Able Children* (NFER–Nelson, 1984).

7

Calculators

CURRENT PRACTICE

Electronic calculators are now a feature of everyday life. A survey, carried out in March 1984, of the new technology available to third-year junior school children in Cambridgeshire and the adjoining counties showed 62 per cent of boys and 49 per cent of girls as having their own calculator. Today the percentages will no doubt be much higher, and it can be expected that many infant school children will also have access to a calculator. As a result the calculator cannot be ignored and must play an integral part in the day-to-day teaching in the primary classroom.

An indication that the actual use of calculators in the teaching of mathematics in the last few years has been sporadic can be gleaned from the HMI report *Primary Education in England* (1978),[1] where no mention whatsoever is made of calculators. Her Majesty's Inspectors had this to say in their guideline document *Mathematics 5–11*[2]:

Any suggestion that children in primary, or indeed, secondary schools should use electronic calculators is often opposed on the ground that it is likely — some would say certain — to have an adverse effect on the acquisition of sound computational skills. However, to use this argument is to fail to take account of the opportunities that the calculator offers as a teaching aid. This is a point which is at present considered by too few teachers. Such systematic classroom studies as are currently available suggest that, far from undermining skills in basic computation, proper use of the calculator can help and encourage children to develop and improve skills.

Further, in the booklet *Agenda for Action,*[3] produced in 1980 by America's National Council of Teachers of Mathematics it was explicitly recommended that mathematics schemes should take full advantage of the power of calculators and computers at all levels. More specifically, the Council recommended that:

> All students should have access to calculators and increasingly to computers throughout their school's mathematics programme. Schools should provide calculators and computers for use in primary and secondary school classrooms. Schools should provide budgets sufficient for calculator and computer maintenance and replacement costs. The use of electronic tools such as calculators and computers should be integrated into the core mathematics curriculum. Calculators should be available for appropriate use in all mathematics classrooms, and instructional objectives should include the ability to determine sensible and appropriate uses. Calculators and computers should be used in imaginative ways for exploring, discovering and developing mathematical concepts and not merely for checking computational values or for drill practice.

The Cockcroft Report is quite clear on the place of the calculator in the primary school:

> Some development work on the use of calculators in the primary years is going on at the present time. In our view, more is needed to consider both the use of calculators as an aid to teaching and learning within the primary mathematics curriculum as a whole and also the extent to which the arithmetical aspects of the curriculum may need to be modified. We believe that priority should be given to this work and to providing associated in-service training for teachers.

Major development work related to the calculator is an integral part of the PRIME project mentioned earlier. This project will, it is hoped, prepare the way for teachers and children to gain confidence in the use of calculators in the primary years.

So, as can be seen from the reports, there is a greater awareness now of the calculator, but along with this are certain fears on the part of teachers.

The Open University report *Calculators in the Primary School*[4] reveals the three most commonly expressed fears of the use of the calculator. Teachers said: 'The main job we have to do in mathematics in the primary school is to give the children a firm grounding in the four rules and number. I'd be afraid that the calculator would undermine their basic arithmetic and they wouldn't bother to learn their tables.'

In addition to the effect on the children's learning there is also evidence given in the report of a fear of the calculator itself. 'I would never use one normally and I would be immediately out of my depth if one of the children asked me a question about it.' Further, 'I can see that the calculator is here to stay and there is a place for it in school but I haven't even begun to grasp its huge potential and the prospect of completely rearranging our maths teaching is rather daunting.'

Such reactions seem quite natural and understandable when expressed by someone faced with the unknown; but they are also negative, and fortunately not all teachers react in this way.

The following quotes from teachers are taken from one of the newsletters published by the Shell Centre for Mathematical Education[5] concerning a project on the use of the calculator with primary children. The first teacher states: 'I have found them [calculators] very beneficial with slow children. One child in particular has been very motivated in this work, a child who otherwise could not concentrate for more than fifteen minutes at a time.' Another teacher felt 'They are extremely useful in extending practical investigations which would otherwise get totally bogged down with heavy calculations.'

A more general effect of the use of calculators was described as follows: 'With very many children I have found that it creates a more confident and positive attitude towards mathematics.' One primary school headteacher was hopeful that calculators would allow teachers 'To present an alive and exciting world of maths to primary school children without losing sight of the basic numeracy which many people feel is important'.

IMPLICATIONS FOR THE CURRICULUM

In many schools at present mathematics is taught without the aid of calculators, and it is acknowledged that the use of them will prove precisely that — an **aid** for both teachers and pupils. Current classroom studies such as those included in the Durham Project suggest that, far from undermining the acquisition of basic computational skills, the proper use of calculators can help and encourage children to develop and improve skills.

Both the Open University research and the Durham Junior Pilot Study[6] have listed the following areas of the curriculum which can be aided by the use of calculators: an understanding of the four rules of arithmetic and their interrelationships; the denary system and place value; an understanding of decimal notation and the relation of decimals to vulgar fractions; negative numbers; pattern investigation and generation; number bonds.

In the early 1980s it was thought that the content of the curriculum could not change significantly but that the order of teaching various skills and concepts would possibly have to be carefully reviewed, but now the traditional pencil-and-paper calculation methods are under considerable threat. It is usual for calculator methods to be employed outside school for most practical calculations, especially with numbers of more than two digits. What is being advocated now is a radical examination of the whole of the number work taught in the primary school and a questioning of the value of the traditional algorithms for doing sums.

Benefits to the curriculum

It is often asked 'What are the benefits of the calculator to the curriculum?' and 'Is it worth while?' In response to these implied criticisms the Open University report gives the following list of benefits which emerge from their research:

'Provides the correct answers'

Although it provides the correct answer to whatever operation is fed into the machine, I have known occasions when the child has said, 'The calculator must be wrong.' Realising that such a thing cannot happen, the child then studies what has gone wrong. This leads the pupil to question his or her keying in of data, judgement as to which process is required, and operational skills — surely a great step forward.

'Enables attention to remain on the problem'

The use of the calculator allows the setting of more realistic problems because the child is enabled to manipulate large numbers and decimals with ease. The calculator thus allows the child to concentrate on the problem-solving aspect instead of being preoccupied with the arithmetic.

'Gives confidence to try specific cases'

There is evidence that as children's confidence in the use of the calculator grows they will attempt further mathematical tasks without fear — tasks they would probably find too difficult or cumbersome using pencil and paper.

'Motivates children to engage in mathematical activity'

There is no question that children like using calculators. All the research into the use of the calculator in the school has stated that the calculator provided considerable motivation at all ability levels. As mathematics still has a reputation for being unpopular, then the possibility that the calculator can affect attitudes deserves serious consideration. It is of special interest that the teachers using the calculators believed that the machines not only improved attitudes towards mathematics lessons in general but specifically improved interest in problem-solving.

'Acts as a catalyst for new mathematical learning'

There are many occasions when the machine acts as a catalyst for new learning. Sometimes keying in incorrect information has produced a negative number in the answer display. This has led to a discussion of directed numbers. Or the machine has introduced the decimal point, and this has made the child ask, 'What are decimals?' The child can on occasion be asked to find out the effect of such keys as $\frac{1}{x}$, x^2, $\sqrt{x}$ and so on. These extra facilities do not seem to confuse or distract children; in fact, they seem to act as a spur to acquiring further knowledge. The calculator can inspire children to think further about the basis of their calculations.

'Provides a very useful diagnostic aid'

When children's understanding of a topic is being assessed by a test or examination, the format used is generally very similar in presentation and content to that used in the teaching of the topic. As teachers are aware, assessments can often test memory rather than understanding. Using the calculator to solve problems, the teacher can readily assess, by watching the child as he or she sets up his or her own questions on the calculator, whether or not there is complete understanding. The format used on calculators to solve a certain problem is not necessarily that which is used with the pencil-and-paper method, so a complete understanding of the processes needed is required of the child.

The choice of calculator

There does not appear to be any single type of calculator which is an outstanding best choice for work with primary children, and with technology changing so quickly new models appear on the market with great frequency. The following features are ones to be aware of when considering the purchase of a particular model for classroom use:

(1) Ensure that the display is liquid crystal, with at least eight digits and floating decimal point and memory-in-use and battery-weak indicators. This will be clear to see and provide a meaningful working display.

(2) Keys should be well spaced, of a reasonable size for young fingers and have a positive (click) action.

(3) A constant memory function is useful when building up number patterns, tables, and so on.

(4) Good 'off', 'on' and 'clear' keys, together with automatic power-down facility after a period of inactivity are almost essential.

(5) Arithmetical logic — rather than algebraic logic — is preferred, that is, $3 + 4 \times 2$ should yield 14 and not 11. In other words, the calculator should perform operations in the sequence in which they are keyed in.

(6) Rounding off $2 \div 3$, for example, should yield 0.6666666

not 0.6666667. The second round-up result, whilst being a more accurate answer, destroys pattern and can lead to confusion.

(7) Calculators containing $\sqrt{x}$, x^2, $\frac{1}{x}$ functions can be useful especially for older primary children to explore. There is no sense in obtaining expensive scientific calculators at this stage.

(8) Negative indicator should be in front of and adjacent to digits in display — not behind the digits or to the extreme left of the display as in some machines.

Use in the classroom

Most commercial mathematics schemes currently available were produced some years ago, before calculators had been identified as a real aid to mathematical learning in the primary school. Newer schemes will doubtless include calculator use as an integral part of the development, but the task facing the majority of teachers at present is one of finding ways of introducing the calculator into daily use alongside well-established routines. There are an increasing number of books and sets of worksheets which provide suggestions as to how this can be done. If children are to bring their own calculators for use in school, teachers must be aware of the differences between various types of machine and the fact that some materials require the use of a specific model of calculator in order to complete the prescribed task successfully. The following examples of calculator activities can be performed successfully on any eight-digit display calculator.

Calculator activities

(1) Use your calculator to work out the numbers in the three sequences:

8×8	9×9	6×6
88×88	99×99	66×6
888×888	999×999	$666 \times ($
8888×8888	9999×9999	$6666 \times$

Look at the pattern in each sequence and w answers to:

88888 × 88888, 99999 × 99999, 66666 × 66666.

Here the calculator provides the child with a means of investigating the pattern in each sequence, but the answer to the last question has to be deduced because the eight-digit display is not sufficient to give a direct result.

(2) Three consecutive numbers multiply to give 635970. See how many 'goes' you need to get the three numbers.

First try

41 × 42 × 43 =	74046	Too small
73 × 74 × 75 =	405150	Still too small
105 × 106 × 107 =	1190910	Too big
92 × 93 × 94 =	804264	Too big
84 × 85 × 86 =	614040	Close
85 × 86 × 87 =	635970	Correct

Try these: 35904, 110544, 124950, 21924.

This type of exercise encourages children to manipulate numbers and to think logically.

(3) Complete this sequence by showing which numbers were added on or taken away at each stage.

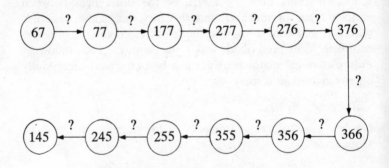

Check with your calculator.
(Do this with the child operating at a mental level and then using the calculator as a check.)

(4) Put in + or − signs so that:

		123	45	67	89			= 100
	123	4	5	67	89			= 100
1	2	34	5	67	8	9		= 100
12	3	4	5	67	8	9		= 100

This example could be undertaken without the use of a calculator but would then probably be rather boring.

(5) Complete

$68^2 =$

$80^2 =$ ◯

The digits in both square numbers are all ◯

There are two more four-digit squares with this property. Which are they?

Find any four-digit squares having only odd digits.

Here, the calculator is a means of searching through a range of square numbers to find the 'even' squares.

REFERENCES

1. DES, *Primary Education in England, A Survey by HM Inspectors of Schools* (HMSO, 1978).

2. DES, *Mathematics 5–11, A Handbook of Suggestions by HM Inspectors* (HMSO, 1979).

3. National Council of Teachers of Mathematics, *Agenda for Action* (National Council of Teachers of Mathematics, 1980).

4. Open University, Mathematics Education Group, *Calculators in the Primary School* (Open University Press, 1982).

5. A.W. Bell *et al.*, *A Calculator Experiment in the Primary School* (Shell Centre for Mathematics Education) (Nottingham University, 1978).

6. C. Jones, *Using Calculators with Junior Children* (Durham County Report, 1980).

FURTHER READING FOR IDEAS AND MATERIALS

Birmingham Mathematics Resource Centre, *Calculator Journey*, Mathematics Resource Centre (Birmingham, 1982).

Keystrokes, *Calculator Activities,* (Addison-Wesley, 1982).

Leapfrogs Group, *Calculators* (Action Book) (Tarquin Publications, 1977).

J. Lewis and H. Davies, *Pocket Calculator Book* (Usborne, 1982).

London Borough of Merton, *Some Lessons with Calculators* (Merton LEA, 1984).

Nuffield Mathematics Group, *Electronic Calculators* (Longman, 1984).

L. Rade and B.A. Kaufman, *Adventures with your Pocket Calculator* (Penguin, 1980).

Resources for Learning Development Unit, *Some Lessons with Calculators,* Calculator Activity Cards (Resources for Learning, 1984).

A. Rothery, *At Home with your Calculator,* calculator puzzles (Nelson-Harrap, 1980–81).

The Durham Project, *Calculator Maths 9–13* (Ward Lock, 1984).

K. Tyler and H. Burkhardt, *Calculator Maths* (Blackie, 1984).

8

Microcomputers

COMPUTERS IN THE CLASSROOM

The microcomputer is now a standard piece of equipment in the primary school, although the number in each school varies tremendously. Microcomputers are beginning to have an influence on the teaching of mathematics, as predicted in the Cockcroft report:

There can be no doubt that the increasing availability of microcomputers offers considerable opportunity to teachers both to enhance their existing practice and also to work in ways which have not hitherto been possible. In particular, the availability of a visual display offers many possibilities for the imaginative pictorial presentation of mathematical work of many kinds.

Elsewhere in the report we are warned that the possession of a microcomputer

does no more than make available an aid to teaching which if it is to be properly exploited, requires teachers to have the necessary knowledge and skill and who have been supplied with, or have had time to prepare, suitable teaching programs. It does however also provide a valuable resource of which individual pupils can make use and from which some are likely to derive considerable benefit.

The national Micro Electronics Project, which came to an

end in 1986, did a great deal to help prepare teachers to use the microcomputer in the classroom. Specially related to mathematics is the in-service pack *Primary Maths and Micros*, released in 1984.[1]

Considering the wide range of programs available for the support of mathematics teaching in the primary school and the in-service back-up available, it is disappointing to find that in some schools a large number of the teaching staff are either unaware of these resources or, if aware, fail to use them.

There may be many reasons for this poor response but three factors seem to play a large part in putting potential users off: firstly, cassette-loaded microcomputers present many difficulties; secondly, many programs are of very poor quality; thirdly, there are few back-up resources to go with most programs.

The technical problems connected with cassette-loading can be reduced by changing to a disc-loading system. While a disc system is more expensive, the saving in teacher and child time is considerable.

The variable quality of programs is a major concern, although many teachers are unclear about how to evaluate the programs they are using. As implied in the second quotation from the Cockcroft report, the microcomputer is no more than an aid to teaching and it is to be expected that the use of a microcomputer will lead to an enhancement of learning. If there is no enhancement, the use of the aid should be questioned. The following questions may be useful in identifying the criteria against which a computer can be evaluated.

Program evaluation

(1) Does the program in question exploit the talents of the computer in order to assist the teacher? The talents may include graphical display, flexibility of response, time control, animation, randomisation, speed and so on.

(2) Is the program 'user-friendly'?

(3) Does the program present a challenge to the children?

(4) Is the program useful in generating conversation?

(5) Does the program provide an opportunity to absorb know-

ledge and techniques not featuring sufficiently in the day-to-day activities of the pupils?

(6) Is the program a resource which helps the teacher to develop real mathematical ideas for the pupils at their own level?

(7) Does the program provide a chance for children to learn more about working together in solving problems and presenting their findings?

The criteria for evaluating textbooks and schemes of work discussed in Chapter 11 can also be examined and, if found applicable, adapted for use with computer programs.

Unfortunately, many programs which are now available do not rate very highly against this set of criteria. It is a matter of some urgency to identify really good programs and have a clear idea of how they can be used in the classroom. It is obviously vital to ensure that the computer program is used in a sensible context and that if additional resources are needed before, during or after the program is used, these are available. Let us now consider the different kinds of computer program and how they can be used in the classroom.

Types of program

The MEP booklet *Teaching Style and Program Design*[2] identified six different types of program: neutral, investigatory, competitive, cornucopean, diagnostic and expository. Although there are programs which fit neatly into each category, there are many which may be classified under two or more headings.

Neutral programs

With the neutral program, the computer is almost an electric blackboard used to reproduce data, draw graphs, perform calculations, display geometrical properties and so on. The high-resolution graph display enables some aspects of mathematical work to be demonstrated in ways which previously would have only been possible with film. For example, the program HALVING illustrates many of the ideas included in the two well-known films *Dance Squared* and *Notes on a Triangle*. The screen retains a square as a starting-point but includes a sequence of changes brought about within the square. The sequence can be stopped for closer examination and discussion. It leads to ideas such as conservation of area, names and properties of plane shapes, symmetries and fractions.

EUREKA is a program where the display shows the level in a bath of water being changed according to certain features. By studying the changes in the level of the bath water, the user is invited to interpret the model and to guess what features are being changed. It is difficult to provide similar opportunities without a computer.

Neutral programs may be used as the basis for a lesson controlled by the teacher or in order to illustrate a point in an ordinary lesson, perhaps for only a brief period.

Investigatory programs

With the investigatory program, the teacher is provided with a system to explore with a class or with a group of pupils. The teacher may be able to control the system so that he or she knows what the class are looking for or may decide to work with the children so that no one knows the solution. Such programs provide a powerful bridge between abstract concepts and applications.

The program SNOOK displays a snooker table and provides the facility of simulating certain paths for a ball on a snooker table. The program might be used with older primary children in order to discuss a pencil-and-paper investigation that they have done for themselves.

An investigation of a different kind for younger children is provided with programs such as MAGIC GARDEN, in which pupils are required to discuss clues and develop strategies for moving towards a determined goal.

Open-ended investigations are provided in a set of programs available from MUSE, in which the user is offered a choice of different layouts of the hundred square for working with addition or subtraction patterns. There is no solution to be found and the motivation comes from the search for interesting patterns.

In these three examples the computer is able to establish a link between abstract ideas and real application. There are many other programs which allow the computer to analyse and display real data. Programs such as FACTFILE provide a structured model for information storage, sorting and retrieval.

Competitive programs

The potential offered by the computer makes it an excellent tool for setting up a whole range of games and puzzles. Some are available to test and reinforce concepts and skills and also encourage the development of mathematical strategies. SIZE-GAME is a program presenting a simple game about place value and probability. Essentially the object of the game is to arrange three digits to give the largest possible number. This kind of game can produce a great deal of discussion and be used with a wide age range of children, from top infants to secondary. The computer is an infinitely patient opponent to any level of skill and ability.

Many traditional games of all kinds can be simulated on the computer, and this can add a new dimension of interest. Some success has been achieved in the teaching of young children to play chess using a computer program which enables the user to set up any position and ask the computer for a move. REVERSI is a computer game based on the board game Othello. Naturally there is a danger of presenting children with computer versions of traditional games instead of the real thing but sensibly handled the computer program can complement the original game.

Although many teachers regard competitive programs to be mainly for individual and group use it is possible to use them with a whole class.

Cornucopean programs

A large proportion of the mathematics programs available commercially deal with the routine practice of skills, and it is suggested that they can be cornucopean in the sense that they provide a prolific number of examples. It is readily accepted that pupils need opportunities to practise skills and routines recently acquired and to consolidate those they already possess. The computer can provide a variety of practice with a degree of control over the level of difficulty and the timing. Machines such as the Little Professor offer the teacher this kind of support already, without the need to use the computer. It may be that in the future the many books of practice examples which have served the needs of teachers for so long will become partially obsolete as the computer comes to provide a more flexible alternative. Unfortunately at the moment many practice programs are of a poor quality and few provide any diagnostic facility.

Diagnostic programs

Much information is now available about the levels of perform-ance reached in a wide range of mathematical topics. A computer could prove invaluable in helping to diagnose the difficulties children have with these topics. For example, the use of practice programs could be monitored by a computer. The apparatus would be able to identify mistakes and difficulties and provide remedial work, with suitable amounts of practice at appropriate levels of difficulty. On the whole, diagnostic programs are at an early stage of development.

Expository programs

Expository programs are designed in such a way that the program teaches the topic itself, presenting ideas in a simple way and involving pupil activity with specific tasks. In some ways these programs can be compared with the better-programmed learning approaches of the 1960s, though in general they too, like the diagnostic programs, are at an early stage of development.

Programming

In the early days of school computing it was thought that those teachers who wished to use computers in their teaching would be able to write their own programs for demonstration pur-poses. Although there are a few primary teachers who do this, most teachers have neither the time nor the expertise to write programs and so mainly use the programs available commer-cially. However, the programming of a computer is to some extent a mathematical activity, thus some activity related to the actual programs can be regarded as an integral part of a course in mathematics and should be included as part of the primary curriculum. Suitable activities include writing a program, inves-tigating a program, and typing a program in order to further develop a mathematical activity.

Writing a program

Most of the programming done in schools is written in the BASIC language, and there can be some satisfaction in learning the rudiments of the language in order to be able to write simple programs such as the following, which draws the capital letter M:

```
100  MODE 1
200  MOVE 100,100 : DRAW 100,300
210  DRAW 200,100 : DRAW 300,300
220  DRAW 300,100
```

Other possibilities enable the child to learn to program without having to master BASIC. At a simple level, the tank BIG TRACK provides the young child with a good introduction to programming leading to more sophisticated control over small robots such as TURTLE, which moves around the floor in response to written instructions from the child.

Investigating a program

Children can learn a great deal about programming by investigating a prepared program. For example, the M program can be examined to see how other capital letters can be written. Why are some letters easy to produce and others difficult? How can simple shapes such as the square, triangle and oblong be produced?

Investigating the following program allows the child to produce a range of tunes (and sounds). Is there a connection between music and mathematics?

```
 10   REM***TUNE***
 20   FOR I%=1 TO 28
 30   READ P,D
 40   SOUND 1,-12,P,D
 50   SOUND 3,-12,P,D
 60   NEXT
 70   DATA 93,4,89,6,73,2,73,4,89,4,93,8,81,4,93,4
 80   DATA 89,6,73,2,73,4,89,4,81,6,69,2
 90   DATA 53,6,93,2,89,6,73,2,73,4,89,4,93,8,81,4
100   DATA 93,4,89,6,73,2,81,6,69,2,73,12
110   END
```

Typing in a program to further an activity

There are many mathematical activities which can be taken a stage further by allowing the child to type in a suitable program.

For example: POLYGON allows the child to draw any regular three- to twelve-sided polygon; TIMES prints any multiplication table up to 50; and HICOFAC finds the highest common factor of any two numbers.

```
10 REMxxxPOLYGONxxx
20   MODE 1
30 PRINT"I will draw a regular polygon with any"
40   PRINT"number of sides between 3 and 12"
50 INPUT'"How many sides",N
60  IF N<3 OR N>12 THEN 50
70  CLS
80   GCOL 0,RND(3)
90 VDU 29,640;512;
100  MOVE 400,0
110 FOR S=1 TO N
120 X=400*COS(S*2*PI/N):Y=400*SIN(S*2*PI/N)
130 DRAW X,Y
140 NEXT S
150 END
```

```
10 REMxxxTIMESxxx
20 CLS
30 PRINTTAB(0,6);"I will give you any times table up to 50"
40 INPUT '"Which table ";T
50 IF T>50 OR T<1 THEN 40
60 K=INKEY(250):CLS
70 FOR N=1 TO 12
80 PRINTTAB(7);CHR$(141);N;" X ";T;" = ";N*T
90 PRINTTAB(7);CHR$(141);N;" X ";T;" = ";N*T
100 NEXT
110 END
```

```
10 REM***HICOFAC***
20 CLS
30 INPUT"THE FIRST NUMBER IS "A
40 INPUT"THE SECOND NUMBER IS "B
50 PRINT"THE H.C.F. IS";
60 IF A>B THEN 80
70 C=A:A=B:B=C
80 A=A-B
90 IF A=B THEN 110
100 GOTO 60
110 PRINT A
120 IF A=1 THEN PRINT "THESE ARE CO-PRIME NUMBERS"
130 END
```

REFERENCES

1. MEP Primary Projects, *Primary Maths and Micros* (MEP: Microelectronics Education Programme, 1984).
2. H. Burkhardt, R. Fraser, C. Wells *Teaching Style and Program Design* (Council for Educational Technology, 1983).

PROGRAMS MENTIONED

HALVING: Primary Maths and Micros, MEP.
EUREKA: Microprimer 2, Techmedia.
SNOOK: Microsmile, Centre for Learning Resources.
MAGIC GARDEN: 4Mation.
MUSE: Micro Users in Secondary Education. A selection of suitable programmes available from this source.
FACT FILE: Cambridge University Press.
SIZEGAME: Primary Maths and Micros, MEP.
REVERSI (also Othello): Mape Software (Mape).
TURTLE: Supplied by Valiant.

FILMS

Dance Squared and *Notes on a Triangle*, National Film Board of Canada (National Audio Visual Aids Library).

ELECTRONIC AIDS

Little Professor: Texas Instruments.

9

Problem-Solving and Investigation

DIFFICULTIES WITH PROBLEM-SOLVING AND INVESTIGATION WORK

One of the most frequently quoted sections in the Cockcroft report is Section 243, which deals with teaching strategies. Here it is stated that opportunities for investigational work, appropriate practical work and problem-solving, including the application of mathematics to everyday situations, should be available to all children.

Although some teachers may only pay lip-service to the idea of practical work, there is a general understanding that this is a necessary component of mathematics teaching in the primary classroom while investigational work and problem-solving are relatively new demands.

One immediate difficulty teachers encounter when considering problem-solving and investigational work is of definition. It is not clear from the Cockcroft report what distinction there is between the two terms. Fortunately, Her Majesty's Inspectors have given us a working distinction, in *Mathematics from 5 to 16*:

> It is useful to think of problem-solving as being a convergent activity where pupils have to reach a solution to a defined problem, whereas investigative work should be seen as a more divergent activity. In an investigative approach pupils are encouraged to think of alternative strategies, to consider what would happen if a particular line of action were pursued, or to see whether certain changes would make any difference to the outcome. In fact, it might be through an investigative approach to a problem that a solution emerged.[1]

So what is being recommended is an open-ended approach to learning where pupils are required to find their own methods of working, select information, think clearly and independently, and use the mathematics they already know intelligently and apply it to unfamiliar and challenging situations. This is a very different view of problem-solving from that offered by many authors of mathematics courses when providing lists of written problems which only offer practice of a skill which has just been learnt.

There is a danger that problem-solving may be thought of as a separate part of the mathematics curriculum and as such be taught at set times within the week, so that at other times within the week 'proper' mathematics is taught. This kind of development would be regrettable. If problem-solving is to be effective it must lead to a fundamental change of attitude on the part of the teacher, who will disregard the stranglehold of the commercial scheme of work and be determined to seize opportunities for developing and following through mathematical work: by exploring the environment; by making use of everyday situations such as the home, the school, travel and shopping; by making use of other areas of the curriculum such as art, music and movement; by the use of projects; by calculator and computer work; work involving puzzles and games, and so on. In this way there will be little differentiation between problem-solving and the remainder of the mathematics curriculum. Children pursuing such a problem-solving approach should be more confident and well able to apply their mathematics to everyday situations.

Let us now look at some examples of how this can be undertaken in the primary classroom.

Mathematical investigations in the environment

Here are some starting-points for this kind of investigation which can be used by children of different ages and ability:

Measurement and maps

How far? Where is X? How far to walk? How big? The use of yourself to estimate lengths. Sketch maps; sketch diagrams. Estimation of angles and distances. Maps in general.

Where you live

House names and numbers. Name as function of building or natural feature. Letter direction; postal code.

Services in the home/at school

Electricity. How does it reach you? Different appliances; groupings. The meter. Nearest power station; national grid. Amount used.

Water. Where does it come from? Position of stop tap; capacity of storage tank; amount used in a day, a week, a year. Is water taken from a river or a reservoir? Running tap–no plug–bath–problem.

Gas. Where does it come from? Type of gas; capacity of gas-holder. Meter; amount used.

Sewage. Where does it go?

Telephone. Telephone numbers: all-figure or exchange and number. How does the dial 'transmit' the number along the wires?

How to use STD: flow diagrams. Where are the nearest call-boxes to your house? Is there an adequate number of boxes? Show the provision of boxes on a sketch-map of the area. Where is the telephone exchange? Where does the wire connecting your home lead to?

Television and radio. Kinds of aerial needed for different kinds of television. Number of channels. Nearest transmitting stations: BBC, ITV, local radio. Can everyone in Britain obtain four channels (BBC1, BBC2, ITV, Channel Four)?

Services

What services come to your door: post, milk, newspapers, refuse, window cleaning, bread, vegetables, meat, fish?

Post. How far does the postman walk each morning? What is the route which includes your house? Is every house on one such route? (Include a visit to the local post office.)
How is mail sorted? Locate the pillar-boxes in your area. When

were the boxes put in this present position? (Insignia on door.) Is the provision of boxes adequate? When are letters collected?

Churches

Where are the local churches (and other places of worship)? What religions are represented? What area is covered by each place of worship?

Transport

Roads. Different kinds of surface. How wide are roads in your area? Can two cars pass? Can cars park? Is your street lit at night? How far apart are the lamp-posts? When and how do lights come on at night, and when do they go off in the morning? How many different kinds of street lights are there in your area? What type is the most effective? Which casts the greatest pool of shadow, and which the least?

Cars. Where in your area can people park their cars? What is the capacity of each car park? Locate garages and filling stations on a map. What services do they offer? What brands and grades of petrol do they sell?

Buses. Mark bus routes on a map. How far is it from your house to a bus stop? Is the positioning of bus stops adequate for the area? Can you produce a better bus route? How often do the buses run, and where can you go? Examine the scale of fares on the different routes. How do they compare in value? (How do you define value?)

Where is the nearest long-distance coach station? What companies run services? Where to? How often?

Are there any pick-up points between your home and the coach station? How long does it take to get to other major towns by bus? Show these on a 'time map'.

Rail. Where is your nearest station? Is it a branch or main-line? If on a branch line, is there a local train service? If so, what other areas in the locality can be reached by this service. Show the service on a topological map (like the map of the London Underground).

What transport facilities are offered by the local station? Examine the inter-city routes and see how 'near' various other towns are.

Port and Docks (examples refer to Newcastle). What special facilities does Newcastle offer? What boats and ships come in? What are their countries of origin? What cargoes are brought in and taken out? How is the incoming cargo distributed?

Show how the port is linked to other means of transport. At what point is the river tidal? How does this affect access for ships?

What buoys, beacons, lights are there?

Are there any ferries in operation? When was the service started? How many people and what goods are carried.

River (examples refer to the River Tyne). How many bridges are there across the Tyne? When was each bridge constructed?

What materials were used? Are the bridges different, or do they have unusual features? Sketch each bridge, estimating the height and weight. What kind of intensity of traffic is carried over each bridge?

Examine the flow of traffic across the bridge and access to each bridge using maps.

Air. How near is the nearest airport? How many runways has it? Examine the noise levels in the vicinity of each runway and check whether any housing is in the flight path.

What scheduled services does it run — where to and where from? (Compare the time element with that for rail and/or bus travel.) How many different airlines use the airport? What is the largest type of aircraft it can handle? Find the number of passengers and amount of freight carried in each month and compare with those of other airports. Is the airport affected by weather?

Locate any disused airstrips in the locality (using Ordnance Survey maps). How do they compare in size to the airport? What is the relation of the length of runway to the type of aircraft using it (if there is one)?

Routes. Choose places 100 and 200 miles away. Plan how you might get there using either public transport (bus, train, air or a combination of the second and third) *or* a car.

How do the routes compare with regard to cost (number of people travelling as variable), time, convenience?

The above is almost a complete mathematics programme for the primary school.

Mathematical project

Often investigational work will feature prominently in a project devoted to a particular subject. In the example, the project on money undertaken by a class of ten-year-olds developed to such an extent that virtually every area of the curriculum was involved. The plan (see p. 90) indicates in skeleton form the range of topics undertaken, and the list of activities shows some of the investigations which were included as part of the project.

Activities

(1) Keep an account for four weeks of all the money you spend.

(2) Make a list of the greatest number of different grocery items you can buy for exactly £5.

(3) Make a list of as many things as you can, with prices, on which your parents have to spend their money.

(4) Why is it necessary for us to have bank notes and coins?

(5) Hire purchase. Find out the deposit and the cost of the total weekly payments to be made if you bought on hire purchase: (a) a bicycle; (b) a transistor radio; (c) a record player. Once you have done this, calculate how much you save in each case by paying cash.

(6) How did people trade before money was invented? Can you give some examples of what was used instead of money?

(7) Paper money: state its real value. What colour and size are banknotes? What is written upon them?

(8) How is it difficult for money to be forged?

(9) Discover as much as you can about the Royal Mint.

(10) Make rubbings of as many different British coins as you can. Arrange these in chronological order. Do you notice differences in design?

(11) On a map of the world, mark the different countries listed on the blackboard and name the currency of each country.

(12) Write a story about a miser.

(13) Write a story about a spendthrift.

Plan

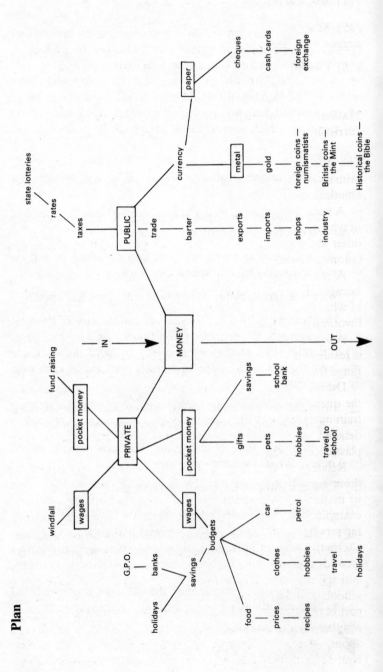

(14) What makes a country rich?

(15) Make a list of poor countries and rich countries. Can you suggest why they are poor and rich?

(16) Poverty: can you discover examples of it in history?

Mathematical investigations from other parts of the curriculum

The following examples, originating in other areas of the primary school curriculum, led to some very meaningful mathematical investigations.

A visit to the Roman fort in South Shields raised the question of why the Romans used squares. This led to an enquiry of what other shapes could be used for building, mosaic work, tessellations and design.

A study of bees and their hives led to the discovery of the hexagonal cells used for honeycombs. This raised the question of what other regular shapes would be possible and why the bee favoured the hexagon.

Another day of rain despite the good weather forecast during a residential trip led to an enquiry into the accuracy of long-range forecasts and the validity of local weather sayings.

During a technology event involving a model railway layout, the question of how a bridge could be strong enough to carry a train many times as heavy as the bridge was raised. This led to a detailed study of the strengths of various frameworks using plastic, cardboard, metal and balsawood strips.

Related to this kind of cross-curriculum investigation are those suggested by the children themselves. They usually refer to matters of immediate relevance to a particular group. For example, one class, continually frustrated at having to queue at the serving hatch for school lunch, decided to set up a study into alternative ways of distributing food in the dining-room. After a great deal of planning involving measurements, scale diagrams and spatial work, a better system was suggested for use in the school. Another group, bothered by the loss of a substantial part of the playground for a new building, decided to investigate whether there was enough space for each child to be able to run about, with arms outstretched, without colliding with anyone else. Most of the planning took place in the classroom with a proportionate reduction in the number of children used to represent the real problem outside. Eventually scale models were produced and a considerable amount of interesting mathematical work undertaken. Unfortunately, the building in the lost part of the playground went ahead.

Starter problems

It can be useful to have a stock of problems available in the school for teachers to use. Many books and magazines give a suitable range, though number problems tend to dominate. The first two examples are of the convergent type, while the others are more open-ended.

(1) (A variation on an old favourite.) A man has to take a wolf, a goat and some cabbages across a river. His rowing boat has enough room for the man plus either the wolf or the goat or the cabbages. If he takes the cabbages with him, the wolf will eat the goat. If he takes the wolf, the goat will eat the cabbages. Only when the man is present are the goat and the cabbages safe from their enemies. All the same the man carries the wolf, goat and cabbages across the river. How?

(2) If you have two buckets, one holding five litres and one holding three litres, how can you measure out four litres exactly?

(3) What shapes can you make from the following? □ △ ○

(4) Use the digits 1, 2, 3 and at most two operations $+, \times, -, \div$ to make 20, 40, 60 different numbers.

Puzzles and games

Many excellent puzzles and games are now available which involve problem-solving strategies. Some games are worth purchasing, but many, like the two examples outlined below, can be made very quickly for classroom use.

Leapfrog game

(on a nine-square board as shown)

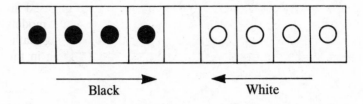

Black counters are placed on one side of the middle hole and white counters on the other. The object is to move the blacks to where the whites are, and vice versa. Black can move one way and white can only move one way. You may only move the piece forward to the adjacent unoccupied square, or jump over to the next-but-one square.

'Add to 15' game

1	2	3	4	5	6	7	8	9

15

In this game, two players take turns to place a counter in one of the boxes 1 to 9. The winner is the first to have any three boxes totalling 15.

The expensive meal

Three men had dinner in a hotel and received a bill for £30. Each of them handed the waiter a ten-pound note. He took the money to the office, where he was told there had been a mistake: the bill should have been for £25, not £30, so he was sent back with £5. On the way back it occurred to him that £5 was going to be difficult to divide between three men, that the men did not know the actual amount of the bill anyway and that they would be glad of any return on the money. So he kept £2 and returned £1 to each of the three men.

Now each man had paid £9. Three times 9 is 27. The waiter had £2 in his pocket, 27 plus 2 is 29, and the men originally handed over £30. Where is the extra pound?

Magic star puzzle

Put numbers in the empty circle so that the sums of four numbers on any line are the same.

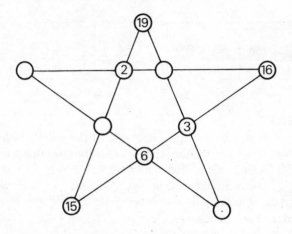

The role of the teacher in problem-solving

The skills necessary for effective problem-solving and investigational work involve a range of teaching techniques and a degree of organisation. Lengthy and involved problems may be better suited to the whole class or groups of children working together with the teacher. Shorter, simpler problems may be better undertaken by children working in pairs or small groups. The teacher may experiment with a problem-solving corner whereby a problem is displayed each week. If the previous weeks' problems are not removed, an increasing number of them will remain on display through the term, thus allowing some pupils to spend a considerable amount of time on a particular problem while others experiment with a wider range at a more superficial level.

The role of the teacher in this kind of activity may be one requiring a shift in emphasis from that of information-provider to question-asker and resource-provider. The children should accept more responsibility for what they do and which course of action they take. If the pupils are to be involved in what they are doing they need to be free of any pressure to finish their work. The activity must be open-ended in the sense that the problem need not necessarily be completed by the end of the lesson and can be continued next time. Pupils must be encouraged to approach a problem in their own way, and a feature can be made of different approaches. This should lead to an increase in creativity and inventiveness.

REFERENCES

1. DES, *Mathematics from 5 to 16*, Curriculum Matters 3, an HMI series (HMSO, 1985).

FURTHER READING

L. Burton, *The Teaching of Mathematics to Young Children Using a Problem-Solving Approach, Educational Studies in Mathematics*, 11 (1980).

L. Burton, *Thinking Things Through, Problem-Solving in Mathematics* (Blackwell, 1984).

A. Straker, *Mathematics for Gifted Children*, Project Report (Longman, 1982). Contains many suggestions for materials and ideas for the classroom.

A. Wood, *Making Changes — Mathematics Curriculum*, Enrichment Packs for Gifted Children (Globe, 1982). A wealth of material.

REFERENCES FOR MATERIALS

Mathematics books, puzzles, sets and shapes

Adler, I.	*Direction and Angles*	(Dobson, 1969).
Adler, I.	*Sets*	(Dobson, 1967).
Bendixk, J.	*Names, Sets & Numbers*	(Watts, 1971).
Bindon, P.	*Numbers and Patterns*	(Macdonald, 1974).
Derry, L.	*Games, Numbers*	(Studio Vista, 1965).
Doig, C.	*Jigsaw Book of Puzzles*	(BBC, 1980).
Edwards, C.	*Sets and Relations*	(Macdonald, 1974).
Froman, R.	*Bigger and Smaller*	(Black, 1972).
Glenn, W.H.	*Fun with Mathematics*	(Murray, 1964).
Grender, I.	*Playing with Number*	(Three, Four, Five, 1976)
Hamilton, B.	*Calculator Fun and Games*	(Fontana, 1982).
	I Can Learn Shapes and Colours	(Hamlyn, 1981).
	I Like Colours and Shapes	(World Int., 1982).
Kilroy, S.	*Young Puffin Quiz Book*	(Puffin, 1982).
Lewis, J.	*Pocket Calculator Book*	(Usborne, 1983).
Marsh, L.	*Let's Discover Shapes and Numbers*	(A & C Black, 1972).
Miller, J.	*How to Fool your Brain*	(Studio Vista, 1975).
Moegenstern, S.	*Metric Puzzles, Tricks and Games*	(Oak Tree Press, 1978).
Murdock, H.	*Big and Little*	(Ladybird, 1980).
	My Own Book of Numbers	(Hamlyn, 1980).

95

O'Brien, T.C.	Odds and Evens	(Black, 1972).
Pluckrose, H.	Shape and Form	(F. Watts, 1979).
	Things Big and Small	(F. Watts, 1974).
Shepherd, W.	The Puzzle Book	(F. Watts, 1971).
Smeltzer, P.	The Circle	(Burke, 1976).
Srivastava, J.	Area	(Black, 1976).
Summers, G.T.	Mind Teasers, Logic Puzzles and Games of Deduction	(Oak Tree Press, 1977).
Trivett, D.H.	Shadow Shapes	(Black, 1976).
Tyler, J.	Brain Puzzles	(Usborne, 1980).
	Number Puzzles	(Usborne, 1980).
	Picture Puzzles	(Usborne, 1980).
	Puzzles	(Usborne, 1980).
Wallace, C.	Zebra Book of Games and Puzzles	(Evans, 1966).
Wingfield, E.	Shapes	(Ladybird, 1978).
Woolcock, P.	Big and Small: A Book of Opposites	(Hodder & Stoughton, 1981).
Youldon, G.	Opposites	(F. Watts, 1979).
	Sizes	(F. Watts, 1979).

Mathematical games

Rubik cube and variations:	Well known
Drive Ya Nuts:	Seven hexagonal nuts with numbered edges to be packed so that touching edges match.
One Way:	Five plastic pieces to arrange as a square.
It's Knot Easy:	Sixteen plastic squares, with 'string' across, to arrange in a square with a continuous loop of string.
Scrambled Egg:	A 3-D jigsaw.
Even Stephen:	10 rods of different lengths have to be placed in 5 holes at varying heights so that the tops of protruding rods lie in a horizontal plane.
Soma Cube:	Seven 3-D pieces to build as a cube.
Cul-de-sac:	Two players start with 2 pawns each on a 12 × 14 board. The aim of the game is to transfer both pawns on to the opponents marked squares.
Mastermind:	Sufficiently well known not to need explanation.
Twixt:	A pegboard game where pegs can be linked with spanners. The object of the game is to build a wall to the opposite side of the board.
Space Lines:	3-D noughts and crosses on a 4 × 4 × 4 board.
Connect Four:	Counters are dropped in to a wall with the object of getting four in any line.

Othello:	Counters are two-sided. There are strategies for capturing the opponents counters and reversing them.
Four Sight:	Tiles are placed on a grid to form the shape of a key-plate. This is a geometrically challenging game, involving rotations and reflections.
Press-ups:	Players depress their own coloured pegs before their opponent.
Quandry:	A board game in which the object is to get a pawn across the board. Moves depend on the positions of the opponents pieces.
Mastermind 44:	In this version, four players simultaneously try to break the hidden code.
Black Box:	A kind of two-dimensional Mastermind. The pattern of atoms has to be deduced from the deflecting of paths of light rays.
Push:	Twenty-five black or yellow balls are placed in a 5 × 5 tray. A ball is pushed according to certain rules, and the object is to form a square of nine balls of your own colour.
Pathfinder:	Grid work and co-ordinates.

Problems

Many local authorities produce booklets containing problem-solving material.

The journals of the Mathematical Association (*Mathematics in School*) and the Association of Teachers of Mathematics (*Mathematics Teaching*) contain many superb problems and articles relating to many issues on mathematics in the primary school.

10

Organisational Matters

In this section it is proposed to consider certain topics related to the organisation of the mathematics curriculum within the school. Good organisational structures are dependent upon a number of factors, and while a particular combination of them can lead to harmony in one school the apparent same mixture can cause chaos in another. What is of crucial importance is the role of the teacher. Regardless of what textbooks are used, what level of equipment is provided and range of microtechnological aids is available, the teacher is the most important resource. So let us begin our view of organisational topics by considering the role of the class teacher.

THE CLASS TEACHER

The Cockcroft Report (Section 12) gives a clear outline of the role of the teacher:

The mathematics teacher has the task of:
enabling each pupil to develop, within his or her capabilities, the mathematical skills and understanding required for adult life, for employment and for further study and training, while remaining aware of the difficulties which some pupils will experience in trying to gain such an appropriate understanding;
providing each pupil with such mathematics as may be needed for his study of other subjects;
helping each pupil to develop, so far as is possible, his appreciation and enjoyment of mathematics itself and his

realisation of the role which it has played and will continue to play both in the development of science and technology and of our civilisation;

above all, making each pupil aware that mathematics provides him with a powerful means of communication.

As mentioned previously, there is also an emphasis on the six aspects of good mathematics teaching at all levels: exposition, discussion; consolidation and practice; practical work; problem-solving; and investigational work — although these do not need to occur at the same time. Most teachers are good at work involving exposition and consolidation but not so ready to adopt problem-solving and investigational approaches. Gentle encouragement will be needed in many schools if newer approaches are to be taken up with confidence. Confidence is, needless to say, the key to successful teaching: if the teacher is not confident the teaching tends to suffer.

It must be clearly recognised that the teaching of mathematics within the school will be governed by the needs of the children and not by the needs of the curriculum. Needless to say, the teacher will be required to cope with a wide range of mathematical ability and will have to use a combination of class, group or individual approaches in order to cater for the needs of each child. There will have to be a balance between oral, written and practical work involving the use of a wide range of resource material. Simplicity and sensibility will be of major significance in organising activities within the class (remember the KISS principle stressed in Chapter 8).

THE MATHEMATICS CO-ORDINATOR

Section 354 of the Cockcroft Report clearly identifies the need for a co-ordinator for mathematics within each primary school: 'The effectiveness of the mathematics teaching in a primary school can be considerably enhanced if one teacher is given responsibility for the planning, co-ordination and oversight of work in mathematics throughout the school.'

The idea of one teacher having responsibility for mathematics within the school is not new, but the term 'co-ordinator' has been used with particular frequency, since the publication of the Cockcroft Report. Few teachers will doubt the wisdom of there being someone with this kind of responsibility, although the notion of a curriculum co-ordinator seems to be advocated in each new primary subject report that appears. Soon every teacher in the primary school will be a co-ordinator for something and there may be no teachers left to be co-ordinated. However, there is possibly a special case to be made for the mathematics co-ordinator when one considers the low level of confidence among teachers as far as mathematics teaching is concerned. The co-ordinator must be someone capable of helping his or her colleagues to increase their confidence in teaching mathematics.

What qualities will this confidence-building mathematics co-ordinator need to have? It is hoped that the person in question will, ideally: be an able mathematician with good solid experience of teaching in the primary school; be interested in and enthusiastic about the subject; have the confidence and respect of his or her colleagues; have attended suitable courses, be up to date in the field of current mathematical activities and able to communicate with other teachers; be able to demonstrate good practice.

Many mathematics co-ordinators have attended appropriate in-service courses, such as that leading to the Mathematical Association Primary Diploma, which aim to develop the individual's skills to do an effective job.

If a school has a mathematics co-ordinator, two things are absolutely essential. Firstly, that person must have the full confidence and support of the head teacher who naturally has the overall responsibility for the whole curriculum (including mathematics) within the school. Secondly, he or she must have a clear job description. In establishing this job description the following must be taken into consideration.

(1) In taking stock of the teaching of mathematics within the school, the co-ordinator will have to consider firstly, *physical* resources such as textbooks, topic books, work cards, material, apparatus, equipment and the storage/distribution of these in the school; and secondly, *teacher* resources, requiring a knowledge of the background and experience of the teachers with whom he/she is working.

(2) The co-ordinator will need to understand and appreciate the different modes of teaching which are being carried out in the school.

(3) He or she will need to find out where teachers need help.

(4) He or she will need to consider the way in which to plan a scheme of work which ensures continuity of the subject throughout the school and the development of each individual pupil.

(5) He or she will need to ensure that there is continuity between schools: between first and middle, between middle and secondary, between primary and secondary, infant and junior.

(6) He or she will need to ensure that there is opportunity to discuss problems with the head teacher.

(7) He or she will need to establish communication with members of staff and to hold formal and informal meetings of teachers.

(8) The contact with the head teacher is essential in order for the head teacher to know the situation and be aware of its limitations in terms of both physical and human resources.

(9) The co-ordinator will need to have contact with co-ordinators in neighbouring schools, head(s) of department in the feed in secondary school(s), co-ordinator(s) in the feeder school(s), local authority mathematics advisory staff and other external agencies.

(10) There will be a need for involvement in the planning of in-service training within the school and possibly within the area.

(11) There will be a need to ensure a sound system of keeping records and the passing on of information between teachers within the school, between schools and to parents.

(12) The co-ordinator should be able to work in the classroom situation alongside colleagues when and where appropriate.

The role of mathematics co-ordinator in the primary school is a difficult and demanding one. It may be that the head teacher is the only member of staff able to take on the job. This is especially true of small schools with few staff. The response to advertisements for the post of mathematics co-ordinator is often very poor, and authorities can be under some pressure to appoint someone even if they are not really suited to the post. Experience has shown that this can be a big mistake and that the school may be better off without a mathematics co-ordinator than with an ineffective one. It is of paramount importance that where a mathematics co-ordinator has been appointed he or she is given the opportunity to do the co-ordinating; it is virtually impossible to carry out the list of responsibilities mentioned and still teach every period of each week. The co-ordinator must have time to devote to this responsible job.

RESOURCES

The following list — by no means exhaustive — is of apparatus which should be available for use in the classroom. Some of the items listed could be made available at a suitably central point in the school to serve more than one class. Some of the smaller items teachers might find useful have not been included here, nor have some kinds of commercial apparatus which can be easily made. An inspection of the catalogues of the leading manufacturers will bring these to light.

Bits and pieces

Scissors, protractors, compasses, rulers, pencils, set squares, felt tip pens

Cardboard of various colours

Paper: brown, coloured, writing, drawing, newspaper, scrap, wallpaper, gummed plain, gummed coloured

Filter papers for practical work with circles (9cm and 11cm in diameter are useful)

Graph paper: 1cm and 2cm squares, rectangular dot arrangements, triangular pattern, hexagonal pattern

String, rope, ribbon, elastic, pins, safety pins, brass split pins, rubber bands, paste, glue, Sellotape, wire

Tins, boxes, containers of various shapes and sizes for shape recognition and model construction

Straws, pipe cleaners

A variety of transparent grids and plain plastic sheets

Plasticine

Collection of rubber stamps and ink pads

Number
Multibase arithmetical blocks. There are a number of alternative sets on the market, and the teacher should compare prices carefully.

Cuisenaire rods (alternatively, Colour Factor or Stern). Useful for fraction work.

Unifix materials: a superb range of apparatus in strong plastic. (There is no need to buy all the ancillary pieces.)

Osmiroid interlocking cubes. These are particularly useful for weight and capacity work. One basic cube weighs 1 gram and has a side of 1 centimetre.

Number dice, fraction boards, different kinds of abacus, 1–100 number squares on duplicated sheets, 1–100 board with matching numerals, 0–100 number line, pegs, counters, shells, beads, pegboard and pegs, basic electronic calculators

Shape

Shape attribute blocks provide a basis for sorting activities and classification work.

Lowenfield poleidoblocks provide a basic set of solids (cubes, cylinders, cuboids, pyramids, discs of various sizes), which are useful for showing relationships between various shapes.

Sets of identical cubes for volume work

Collection of two- and three-dimensional shapes

Meccano strips and Geostrips

Spirit levels

Plane mirrors for work on reflection and symmetry

Tangrams

Measurement

Metre sticks

School rulers in 20cm or 30cm lengths

Measuring tape (m and cm)

Metre trundle wheel, calipers, height measurer

Tape measures, set squares, balances for weighing, spring hook balance, kitchen scales and bathroom scales

Basic set of weights: 1kg, $\frac{1}{2}$kg, $\frac{1}{4}$kg, 200g, 100g, 50g, etc.

Buckets, litre, $\frac{1}{2}$ litre, $\frac{1}{10}$ litre containers

Medicine spoons for 5ml units

Collection of containers for the measurement of volume

Set of cubes with sides measuring 1cm, 2cm and 3cm

Displacement container for volumes of irregular shapes

Sets of shapes for tessellation work

Regular tessellation patterns on acetate sheets for use as overlays

Pendulum (bob and string), egg timer, ten-second timer, metronome, stop-watch, kitchen timers, real clocks, simple clock faces for demonstration and practice, calendars, time-tables, clock-face rubber stamps (twelve- and 24-hour), rocking second timers

Real coins for money work

Library

A range of general books related to mathematics for child use. (See the list at the end of this chapter.)

A range of teacher manuals for reference. (A range of manuals is given in Chapter 4.)

LIAISON

The different kinds of school organisation adopted throughout the United Kingdom means that some pupils will be transferring from one school to the next at the ages of seven, eight, nine, ten, eleven, twelve or 13. The major transfer for most children is that from primary to secondary school, so the following comments will concentrate on this stage although the comments can be adapted for other ages of transfer.

If primary and secondary education are not to be seen in isolation, then successful liaison is important. The needs of the child can only be satisfied if the transfer from one school to the other is effected smoothly. Liaison in mathematics is of course only one aspect of the more general liaison, but because of the sequential way in which the subject is taught it must be given high priority.

Good liaison fosters a great understanding of the methods,

skills and problems of the teachers in different schools. It allows the detailed profile which the primary teacher has built up on each child to be transferred and utilized for the benefit of that child. Primary teachers often feel discontented that the knowledge they have acquired about individual children is lost on transfer to secondary school, and secondary teachers often do not have access to official transfer records (if these exist). Moreover, there is sometimes concern about the consistency of attainment grades given by primary teachers. An absence of feedback from the secondary school on their ex-pupils' progress means that primary teachers are not helped to evaluate their assessments.

Liaison between schools can take many forms, but the most common kind is that which takes place through meetings between head teachers. Such meetings tend to be more concerned with policy and administrative matters than with the exchange of ideas, views and information that characterises teacher meetings. These involve looking at syllabuses and schemes of work, classroom organisation, methods of dealing with able and less able pupils, assessment and so on. Visits to the classroom in different schools helps to provide a feeling for, and a working knowledge of, the other school's problems and methods. Such visits tend to be undertaken by secondary teachers, but they can also be of great value to primary teachers.

Through successful liaison decisions relating to the transfer of information from primary to secondary school should be possible. When pupils transfer they will have achieved different levels of attainment in mathematics. This difference will be most marked in number work. It is essential that the child should be allowed to progress from his or her present stage of development, and if this calls for a radical rethinking of teaching methods in the early stages of secondary school then that rethinking should take place. In the past too many more able children have been bored by the unnecessary repetition of previously mastered skills and too many less able children totally bewildered by having to attempt work in advance of their conceptual readiness. Individual differences must be taken into consideration when planning for the needs of the young secondary child.

LOCAL AUTHORITY SUPPORT

The Cockcroft Report clearly recognises that mathematics is a difficult subject to teach. If this is so, any class teacher in a primary school can expect to receive the maximum possible support from the local authority. This is even more necessary when it is realised that the primary teacher is normally teaching a class every lesson and has no non-contact time with children.

Support from the authority may take a number of forms: visits and advice from the mathematics adviser and/or teacher adviser for mathematics; guidance booklets on aspects of primary mathematics; production of teaching materials; practical assistance in the classroom at the 'chalk face'; school based in-service courses; nomination for local, regional and national courses; affiliation to a national curriculum development project such as PRIME[1]; and so on.

The examples in the Appendix illustrate how a local authority can support the work of the teacher in the classroom by providing opportunities for activities not easily made available by the class teacher or school working in isolation.

REFERENCES

1. PRIME Project: Primary Initiatives in Mathematics Education, School Curriculum Development Committee. Further information can be obtained from SCDC or Homerton College, Cambridge.

BOOKS FOR THE LIBRARY

Allington, R.	*Beginning to Learn About Numbers*	(Raintree, 1979).
Allington, R.	*Beginning to Learn About Shapes*	(Raintree, 1979).
Anno, M.	*Anno's Counting House*	(Bodley Head, 1982).
Bakewell, R.	*Sorting and Matching Shapes*	(Geoffrey Chapman, 1969).
Bakewell, R.	*Sorting and Ordering Shapes*	(Geoffrey Chapman, 1969).
Bradbury, L.	*Counting*	(Ladybird, 1978).
Ball, J.	*Think of a Number*	(BBC, 1979).
Catherall, E.	*Investigating Areas*	(Wayland, 1982).
	Investigating Graphs	(Wayland, 1982).
	Investigating Sets	(Wayland, 1982).

	Investigating Numbers	(Wayland, 1982).
East, H.	*Counting Book*	(Macdonald, 1982).
Edwards, R.	*Counting and Measuring*	(Burke, 1970).
Greenwood, A.	*Numbers*	(Ladybird, 1981).
Hay, D.	*I Can Count*	(Collins, 1977).
Hindley, H.	*Counting Book*	(Usborne, 1979).
Law, F.	*Mouse Count*	(Octopus, 1980).
Marsh, L.	*The Guinness Mathematics Book*	(Guinness Superlatives, 1980).
Murray, W.	*Addition Made Easy*	(Ladybird, 1967).
Nichols, F.	*Shape Play Book 1: Circles*	(Child's Play, 1976).
Nichols, F.	*Shape Play Book 2: Stencils*	(Child's Play, 1976).
Nichols, F.	*Shape Play Book 3: Curves*	(Child's Play, 1976).
Nichols, F.	*Shape Play Book 4: Tangrams*	(Child's Play, 1976).
Oram, S. (ed.)	*Seaside Maths*	(Macdonald, 1973).
	Kitchen Maths	(Macdonald, 1973).
	Circus Maths	(Macdonald, 1973).
	Going Places with Maths	(Macdonald, 1974).
	Farm Maths	(Macdonald, 1974).
	Clothes Maths	(Macdonald, 1974).
	Building Maths	(Macdonald, 1974).
Peppé, R.	*Humphrey the Number Horse*	(Methuen, 1978).
Pluckrose, H.	*Things have Shapes*	(F. Watts, 1978).
Sitomer, H.	*How Did Numbers Begin*	(T. Crowell, 1976).
Smeltzer, P.	*The Rectangle*	(Burke, 1976).
Smeltzer, P.	*The Triangle*	(Burke, 1976).
Smeltzer, P.	*Mathematics Encyclopedia*	(Burke, 1980).
Stables, A.	*Number Practice*	(Schofield, 1981).

11

The Choice of a Mathematics Scheme

THE RANGE OF SCHEMES AVAILABLE

Whatever uncertainties exist with regard to the teaching of mathematics in the primary school, one thing is certain: during the next year or so another primary mathematics scheme will appear on the market. This will compete with *Ginn Mathematics, Nuffield, SPMG, SMP 7–13*, Fletcher, *Peak Beta* and the rest.

A check made in 1980 in one northern education authority revealed 74 different schemes being used in part, or whole, in primary schools. Today teachers are faced with a choice of almost 100 different series of mathematics books, although it must be admitted that some may be out of print and only available from cupboards in certain schools.

Since the pioneering days of Nuffield in the 1960s hundreds of thousands of pounds must have been spent on mathematics books. Schemes have been bought, used and rejected. Some schools offer a real journey down memory lane as one walks down the corridor and passes the Flavel and Wakelam cupboard, the Beta cupboard, the Fletcher cupboard and so on. Some schemes have been simultaneously phased in to all the year-groups in the school at the same time with little regard for continuity.

The reasons why a particular scheme is chosen for a particular school are many and varied. In some schools, a change of head teacher means an automatic change of mathematics scheme. Some authorities adopt a common policy for all schools within the authority with little regard for the needs of the individual school. Sometimes a new scheme is ordered on the recommendation of another school or after a brief inspection of sample material. Teachers attending in-service courses are often introduced to the latest scheme and feel as a result that this is the one which is currently in fashion and so must be ordered. What is clear is that the saying 'One man's meat is another man's poison' can be applied to mathematics schemes.

Let us now consider a framework against which various schemes can be appraised. It will be useful to first establish some ground rules for text evaluation:

(1) Evaluation is intended to help teachers choose a scheme which is best suited to the individual school.

(2) It is not intended to decide upon a 'best buy' for everyone.

(3) Situations will vary tremendously between schools so what is selected in one school may be different to that in another.

(4) Ideally, all the teachers in the school should be involved in the evaluation. It is rarely adequate to leave this job to one person, whether it be the head teacher or the mathematics co-ordinator.

(5) The production of a national league table for mathematics schemes is not intended and would be undesirable.

(6) Whatever mathematics scheme is used in the school it must be the servant of the teacher and not the master. No commercially produced scheme will ever be perfect for an individual school.

(7) The teacher in the school must feel confident in using the chosen scheme.

(8) Before purchasing a new scheme for the school it is essential to know the limitations of the one being phased out. This can be undertaken by applying the same evaluation procedures to the old scheme as will be applied to the new ones being considered.

Framework for evaluation

The school

It is important that the school variables likely to affect the choice of mathematics scheme are clearly identified. These will

109

include: the number of children, classes and teachers; the ethnic composition of the school; the kind of school organisation; the catchment area of the school; local plans between schools for mathematics; facilities in the school.

Description of the materials

It is essential that the teachers involved in the appraisal are fully aware of all the details of the scheme under consideration. Information to be collected here will include: aims and content of the scheme; target population and mode of use suggested by the authors; materials needed in order to implement the scheme, such as calculators, computers, specialist apparatus, duplicator, copier; whether recording and assessment are integral components of the scheme; cost; whether any part of the scheme is disposable and will need repurchasing every year.

Use of materials with children

Before any major scheme is purchased for use in school some of it should ideally have been tried out with the children in the classroom. This can be undertaken by borrowing materials from a neighbouring school, teachers' centre, college library or elsewhere. Alternatively, sample material from the publisher may be used. The evaluation process for materials already in use in the school can be easily undertaken, often from immediate personal knowledge. The evaluation of the use of the materials can best be approached by asking the following questions:

Is the material attractive, enjoyable and colourful?

Is the material easy for the children to handle and suitable for storage, distribution and collection?

Is the material robust?

Does the material encourage the development of skills in investigation, understanding of pattern in mathematics and mathematical order in the environment?

Does the material engage the interest of children and develop a sense of enjoyment of mathematics?

Are the situations described, and imagery used, appropriate to both sexes and pupils from different social and ethnic backgrounds?

Is the presentation of topics logical and clear?

Are pupils encouraged to explain mathematical topics through discussion?

Does the material encourage the use of imagination and creative thinking?

Are there problem situations which: relate to practical activities; require pupils to select appropriate mathematical strategies and techniques; have a range of solutions requiring pupils to exercise analysis and judgement?

Is there a spiral approach to mathematics where the scheme keeps returning to concepts in the advanced form?

Are there sufficient opportunities for reinforcing practical, written and mental skills?

Is any assessment material useful in diagnosing difficulties for the pupils and planning programmes of work?

Do teacher materials provide clear instructions, information about resources, identification of underlying mathematical activities, adequate solutions and consistency with pupil material?

Is the scheme demanding of teacher skills and time in terms of classroom management, further planning, selection and production of supplementary material and mathematical expertise?

Are specific teaching strategies required by the scheme?

Are these strategies compatible with the organisation of the school and with the individual classrooms?

Readability

The major criticism of many schemes is with regard to the language and notation used. One way of gauging the level of difficulty caused by the language in the text is to use a test of readability. Unfortunately, most tests are best used with passages of continuous prose and there is some difficulty when applying them to mathematical texts where prose is heavily interspersed with symbols. Two tests which focus on word length and sentence length are the Mugford Readability Chart[1] and Fry's Readability Graphs.[2]

111

A test which focuses on whether written passages are easy to make sense of as a whole is Cloze procedure.[3]

Cloze procedure focuses on whether or not there are internal clues within passages which help readers to make sense of unfamiliar words. It does this by asking the reader to try to fill in missing words in passages taken from the book.

Steps for Cloze procedure

The teacher should select two or three passages taken from different parts of the book. Each passage should start at the beginning of a paragraph, and contain about 350 words.

Delete every seventh word in each passage, and substitute with a dash; all dashes should be of equal length. An attempt should then be made to recreate the original passage by supplying the missing words.

In assessing the results, firstly reject words not in the original text, even though they may seem commonsense alternatives, to do otherwise affects the reliability of the scoring. Secondly, reject grammatical errors, for the same reason. Thirdly, accept wrong spellings. Work out the number of correct replacements as a percentage of the total number of deletions.

Approximately 60% or more correct: the reader can probably work independently with the text. Approximately 40% or less correct: the text is probably too difficult for the reader, even with teacher help. Between 40% and 60% correct: teacher help will be required, but the text will be useful.

The teacher may find that these percentage levels tend to underestimate the difficulty of mathematical text and so should be interpreted with caution.

A fuller description of the use of readability tests is given by Harrison in the book *Readability in the Classroom*.[4]

Alternative to readability tests

An alternative way of ascertaining levels of difficulty without getting into the complexities of formal readability tests can be followed by attempting to identify key criteria relevant to the issue. This can be done by asking the following questions:

Is the layout clear and uncluttered?

Is the print suitable in terms of size and type?

Are sentences short and simple, using vocabulary which is appropriate to the age and ability of the pupils?

Are mathematical terms introduced with suitable explanations?

Are arguments logically presented and easy to follow?

Is the text broken up into comprehensive units of argument?

Are diagrams and illustrations appropriate to the age and ability of pupils and well placed in relation to the text?

Are there useful subheadings in the text?

Is the material interesting to the pupils?

Is there a useful index?

Decision time

After using the framework to evaluate a particular scheme, the key question of continued use or recommended adoption has to be faced. The criteria identified as part of this framework should provide teachers with sufficient information to answer this question. It will not be necessary for a scheme to score favourably against each item in order to be effective for use in a school. It is up to the teachers in the school to decide on the key criteria they think relevant to their needs in the school, and these will vary from school to school.

The framework for evaluation suggested in this chapter involves teachers in a fair amount of work, and it will be asked whether such activity is worth while. It must be stressed that any decision to introduce a new mathematics scheme into a school involves a large amount of money. It is essential that this decision is based upon a thorough consideration of all the factors involved. The factors discussed here can of course be adopted when considering other types of mathematical material or material relating to other areas of the curriculum.

After the decision

It must be understood by all the teachers in a school that no matter how careful the selection of a scheme may have been and how sensibly it may have been phased into use, that scheme will not be perfect. The scheme must be the servant of the teacher. In too many instances the scheme has been allowed to become the master of the teaching situation in mathematics. New topics should always be introduced to the child by the use of appropriate oral and practical work. Learning mathematics from the printed page is difficult for many children and is developed very slowly. Language problems exist for some pupils in virtually every scheme available. Some of these problems have been discussed in an earlier chapter (see Chapter 6), and it is not the intention to repeat that discussion here but to consider strategies available to the teacher to minimise these. The policy of trying to avoid reading difficulties by preparing work-cards in which the use of language is either minimal or avoided altogether is discouraged in the Cockcroft Report. There, it is suggested that necessary language should be developed through discussion and explanation. However, the majority of children will still be faced, even after discussion and explanation, with some reading from the printed page. Reading problems can be tackled by trying to improve the child's ability to read mathematical text. The following strategies can be adopted:

(1) Examine the mathematical text carefully and colour-code the key words. These words can also be put into a survival vocabulary list.

(2) Locate the technical words used in the text and put these into a dictionary. (Some schemes may have such a dictionary.) Home-produced dictionaries can be simply illustrated.

(3) Make flash cards for the key words in the text. Spelling flash cards used in ordinary language work within the primary school are rarely used in a mathematical situation. Regular mathematics spelling tests can be combined with the flash-card work.

(4) For some topics involving a lot of reading, compose mathematics word pre-tests.

(5) Record difficult text on cassettes and allow the child to listen to the spoken word as well as reading the text.

(6) Isolate the really poor reader and give explanations. Remember that it does not necessarily follow that a poor reader is poor at mathematics.

(7) Adapt the traditional practice techniques used in the teaching of reading to mathematics, for example: unscrambling anagrams; crosswords; finding missing words in a sentence; matching words to definitions or pictures etc.

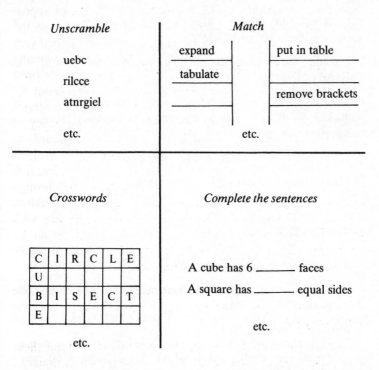

Unscramble	*Match*
uebc	expand — put in table
rilcce	tabulate
atnrgiel	— remove brackets
etc.	etc.

Crosswords

C	I	R	C	L	E
U					
B	I	S	E	C	T
E					

etc.

Complete the sentences

A cube has 6 _____ faces

A square has _____ equal sides

etc.

Contact the language expert in your own school for further suggestions and help.

Teacher-produced material

Whatever commercial mathematical texts are used, teachers tend to produce their own materials as a complement or in some cases as a direct replacement. Invariably, home-produced material in the primary classroom takes the form of work sheets or work cards, although some teachers have produced interesting booklets on particular topics. Reading difficulties can be minimised by adopting the following suggestions:

(1) Keep to the present tense.

115

(2) Avoid clumsy conditional language, such as: If a packet of sweets costs 24p, how much would twelve packets cost?

(3) Avoid using different words for the same thing: table, chart, matrix, diagram.

(4) Avoid many of the extremely ambiguous common words such as 'difference' and 'light'.

(5) Avoid difficult words if they are not essential to the purpose of the text.

(6) Avoid using unnecessary technical words where possible. If technical words are essential they must be carefully introduced and repeatedly revised.

(7) Use short sentences and simple language.

(8) Avoid unnecessary expository material.

REFERENCES

1. L. Mugford, A New Way of Predicting Readability, *Reading*, 4 (1970).

2. E.B. Fry, 'The Readability Graph Validated at Primary Level', *Reading Teacher*, 22 (1969).

E.B. Fry, 'Fry's Readability Graph: Clarifications, Validity', *Journal of Reading*, 21 (1977).

3. M.A. Hater and R.B. Kane, 'The Cloze Procedure as a Measure of Mathematical English', *Journal of Research in Mathematics Education*, 16 (1975).

4. C. Harrison, *Readability in the Classroom* (Cambridge University Press, 1980).

FURTHER READING

D. Lumb *et al.*, *Primary Mathematics: Critical Appraisal Document* (Longman, 1984).

H. Shuard and A. Rothery, *Children Reading Mathematics* (John Murray, 1984).

12

Assessment

Assessment is an essential part of the teaching process, although, as we are reminded in Section 5.1 of *Mathematics from 5 to 16*,[1] it should develop out of the curriculum, its aims, objectives, criteria for content and approaches and not the reverse. It should not be an end in itself but the means of providing information which can form the basis of future action. Assessment will be taken to include the use of formal and informal tests, continuous recording of mathematical progress and profile sheets as well as the incidental assessment undertaken by the teacher through discussion, questioning and checking of work done each day.

TESTING

Reference has already been made in previous sections to the use of tests for diagnosing learning difficulties in mathematics and the identification of mathematically more able pupils. Moreover, it is found that tests are used for the following purposes in the primary school (though there will, of course, be many more):

(1) comparing a school's standard with accepted national norms;
(2) comparing one school year with another;
(3) grouping children within a class;
(4) grading pupils within a year group;
(5) checking mastery of particular concepts of skills;

Different kinds of tests

(6) providing information on transfer from one school to another;

(7) screening children.

It will be useful to briefly consider the different kinds of test available to the teacher.

Norm-referenced tests

This kind of test aims to measure the pupil's general mathematical ability or attainment, usually giving the result as a number (in the case of a standardised test, this will be a standardised score similar to an IQ value) or mathematical age. The result can then be compared with norms relating to different age ranges obtained in national trials. The tests from the series *Mathematics 8–12*[2] are good examples of this type.

Some norm-referenced tests apply only to arithmetic and were presumably popular when number work dominated the primary mathematics curriculum.

General cognitive tests

Some sets of tests include mathematics as part of a general range of academic attainments. They usually produce a range of standard scores relating to each area tested. The *Richmond Tests of Basic Skills*[3] is one such package, producing eleven scores altogether with three relating to mathematics (concepts, problem-solving, reading graphs and tables).

Profile tests

A profile test is one which produces a range of separate scores for different aspects of the test. The *Profile of Mathematical Skills*[4] is one such test where a profile of strengths and weaknesses across a whole range of appropriate mathematical topics is obtained.

Criteria-referenced tests

These tests are designed to check whether a child is able to perform certain prescribed tasks resulting in either a 'yes/no' answer or a level of development. Many checklists produced by local authorities or as integral parts of a commercial scheme are examples of this kind of test. A very detailed list of objectives for primary mathematics has been produced in *Yardsticks*,[5] where a short test is available for each objective.

The *Early Mathematics Diagnostic Kit*[6] is another example of a criteria-referenced test. This is produced especially for young children, whereas the majority of primary tests apply only to the junior years.

WHICH TEST TO USE

- so many ways to assess but no kind of test a teacher would use

The appropriateness of a particular kind of test will be determined by the task to be undertaken. On the whole, norm-referenced tests are more appropriate to the first five uses outlined here, with profile- and criterion-referenced tests being more suited to diagnostic work. The general cognitive tests can be useful in comparing a child's performance in mathematics with his or her performance in other areas within the battery.

A word of caution

SE2
chrispher (clearly)

One note of caution when using tests is to remember that most of them require the child to read and comprehend the test item before answering. What is often being tested is rather more than mathematical ability, and the reading age of the child may significantly affect the performance.

orally talk about size / compared

As a follow-up to the work of the APU some schools are now experimenting with practical testing. This usually involves a one-to-one situation between the pupil and teacher if done formally, but it is possible to test a small group on selected items. Naturally this kind of testing removes the problem of the children having to read the question and allows the teacher to see the child's reaction when an instruction is read.

Some teachers will work in schools where blanket testing has been introduced by the local authority. At best this kind of testing is useful in identifying both successful practice and those schools in need of additional support. At worst it is used by mischievous elected members, governors, parents and others to provide a crude comparison of the mathematical performance of one school with another without any consideration being given to other important factors affecting performance. In general, it is to be hoped that those choosing tests for this purpose will at least ensure that the tests provide as much information as possible and do not concentrate too heavily on certain parts of the mathematical curriculum at the expense of others which are equally important.

Standardised tests, however well chosen and for whatever good intentions they are to be used, measure only certain aspects of mathematical attainment; they do not test perseverance, attitudes, flair, application, creativity, enjoyment and so on. Test results should not be used by themselves but in conjunction with these other factors. This is especially true when children transfer from one stage of schooling to the next.

Curriculum domination

There is a danger that testing can come to dominate the mathematics curriculum in the school to such an extent that teachers teach in accordance with the test content. This tends to result in a whole class approach at the expense of individual or group approaches and an over-emphasis on skill learning.

Tests can be devised by teachers working in the school, and although such tests are not standardised they do have the advantage of fitting in with the work of the individual classroom. These tests should be within the reading capabilities of the children for whom they are intended and can reflect problem-solving and investigational approaches. They can also be made to be of a practical nature, whereas the majority of commerical tests tend to be very much pencil-and-paper exercises.

Over-testing can affect the children's attitude towards mathematics. It is wrong to assume that mathematical ability increases as the frequency of testing increases; in fact, too much testing can do children positive harm. Perhaps tests should carry a government warning 'Can be harmful to children' to alert teachers to the dangers!

Record of progress

If pupils are to be allowed to develop to their full potential, then it is important that a record is kept of the progress of each child in the class. This is particularly vital for children working individually or in small groups. This record must follow the child through the school and be available either in its original or a condensed form to the teachers in the next school on transfer. Because of this it is desirable for the record to be of a standard form throughout the school. It is very cumbersome for each teacher to have an individual record system, therefore the school staff must get together and decide the exact form the record system is to take. Experience has shown that a record system imposed on the staff with little or no consultation has a poor chance of being used successfully in the school.

Ideally the record system should attempt to gauge the child's achievement in mathematics, the development of his or her mathematical ideas and his or her attitudes to mathematics. If children are working from graded work cards they can keep a check of their own progress by crossing off the name on the card against their own names on a list when the card has been completed.

	Susan							
Blue	1	2	3	4	5	6	7	8
Green	1	2	3	4				
Yellow	1	2	3	4	5	6		
Red	1	2	3	4	5			
etc.								

Alternatively, the crossing-off can be done by the teacher. There are obvious dangers in using such a model, but it can provide a simple record of achievement. It can, of course be adapted to meet the needs of kinds of organisation other than the work-card approach.

Children's attitudes towards teaching are of great importance but are very difficult to measure directly. As a result, the opinions of teachers are vital in terms of giving some indication of attitudes, and it is important to allow spaces for comment in all record schemes.

In the following example the child's progress is gauged with reference to a list of key concepts, skills and experiences appropriate to the primary years. It is, needless to say, impossible to include all the stages and list all the items included in a primary mathematics programme on a record card, but the list should be comprehensive enough to give an overall indication of progress. One way of using the list is to ask the teacher to arrange the items as shown in the final part of the example with three columns headed A, B and C alongside. Each item is then ticked and dated under the appropriate column when the child has:

A: an introduction to this concept, skill or experience
B: involvement with this concept, skill or experience
C: consolidation of this concept, skill or experience

	A	B	C	Comments

Number names from 1 to 10
One-to-one correspondence
Recognition of number of
   objects in collection
1, 2, 3, 4, 5, 6, 7, 8, 9, 10 and 0
   (cross out when known)
Recognition of number symbol
0, 1, 2, 3, 4, 5, 6, 7, 8, 9, 10
   (cross out when known)				

Conservation of number Ordering of numbers 1–5, 1–10 Composition of numbers to 10				
Operation of addition (numbers to 10) Operation of take away Operation of difference between				
Complementary addition Number bonds to 10 Number vocabulary 11–20				
Counting on and back to 20 Composition of numbers to 20 Odd and even to 20				
Subtraction to 20 Counting and grouping in 2, 3, 4, 5, 10 Division by sharing Patterns of 2, 3, 4, 5, 10 and 0–99 square Fractional parts: one whole, $\frac{1}{2}$, $\frac{1}{4}$				

Additional items:

Number

Number sequence to 100
Counting on and back to 100
Composition of numbers to 100
Commutative law of addition (i.e. $2 + 3 = 3 + 2$)
Square numbers (1, 4, 9, 16, 25, etc.)

Addition of numbers to 99
Subtraction to 99
Number sequence beyond 100
Counting on and back
Composition of numbers beyond 100

Rectangular numbers
Prime numbers
Counting and grouping in 2, 3, 4, 5, 10, 6, 8
Addition beyond 100 (appropriate recording)
Subtraction beyond 100 (appropriate recording)

Multiplication   (a) by a number less than 10
                (b) by 10
                (c) multiples of 10

Division   (a) by a number less than 10
                (b) by 10

Significance of place value
Consolidation of number bonds to 20
4 basic rules of arithmetic
Problems involving 4 basic rules

Equivalence of fractions, e.g. $\frac{1}{2} = \frac{2}{4} = \frac{3}{6}$ etc.
Tables, multiples and factors
Simple computation with fractions

Extension of place value to decimals ·1, ·01, ·001
Addition and subtraction of decimals
Fraction, decimal, percentage relationships

Analysis of number relationship:
(a) commutative
(b) associative
(c) distributive

Extension of number line in positive and
    negative directions
Multiplication and division of fractions
    (sensible situation)
Directed numbers: multiplication and
    division
Multiplication and division of decimals
Ratio
Powers and indices
Significant figures
Calculating devices

Shape

Sorting out of angular and curved shapes,
    two- and three-dimensional
Comparison — vocabulary development —
    'large' and 'small'
Names of shapes
Dissecting shapes and recombining for mosaics
Recognition of symmetrical shapes
Ability to express shapes (drawing,
    modelling, etc.)

Tessellation with various units
Choosing most suitable unit to cover surface
Extension of language of shapes to include
    parts of a circle
Making and application of right angles
Recognition of angles larger and smaller
    than right angles
Symmetry

Three-dimensional work:
    nets
    naming parts
    naming solids
Two-dimensional shapes:
    properties

Similarity
Congruency
Rotation
Translation
Reflection

Money and shopping

Sorting and recognition of coins
Practical shopping 1p, up to five separate
    pennies

Shopping for items costing more than 1p
Buying more than one item, using
    combinations of coins to 5p

Recognition and value of coins to
    (a) 10p
    (b) 20p
Change involving exchange of coins with
    shopkeeper using
    (a)   5p coin
    (b) 10p coin

Shopping with, and combinations of
    amounts to (a) 20p
              (b) 50p
              (c) £1
Amounts over £1: the use of the dot.
Bills

Measurement

Length

Sorting language
Comparison of two objects — 'shorter',
    'taller', 'longer', etc.
Ordering 3 or more objects
Equality
Filling in length with different measures

Need for standard measurement
Metre, decimetre, centimetre. Fractional
    parts of metre
Estimation of length
Measurement of curves using string, etc.
Conversion of above to linear measure
Perimeter of three-, four-, five- etc. sided
    shapes and circles

Ability to use various measuring
    instruments
Relationship between mm, cm, m, km
Different forms of notation (i.e. $156\,cm =$
    $1{\cdot}56\,m$)

Weight

Sorting language
Comparison of two objects: 'heavier',
    'lighter'
Ordering by estimation (three objects)

125

Ordering with use of balance
Balancing — equal weights

Use of improvised units of weight
Need for standard unit — (gram, kilogram)
Comparison of objects with standard unit
Estimation of weight

Ability to use various measuring
    instruments
Relationship between g and kg
Different forms of notation
Tonne

Capacity

Language from free play
Full and empty
Comparison of two containers — holds
    more/less than
Ordering jars by capacity

Filling large container from smaller
    containers
Sharing contents among smaller containers
Improvised standard units
Need for standard unit (litre, millilitre)
Use of standard measurements
Estimation of capacity

Standard measures l, ml
Ability to use various measuring
    instruments
Relationships between l, ml, and cm^3
Volume of irregular solids by displacement
Volume of cuboids

Area

Conservation of area
Measurement of area (regular and irregular
    shapes) — standard units
Formulae for regular shapes
Hectare

Time

Sequence associated with child's daily
    routines
Appropriate vocabulary including 'fast' and
    'slow'

Timing by rhythmic movement (pendulum, clapping, etc.)
Reading the clock face: 'o'clock' times, 'half past', 'quarter past', 'quarter to'
Days, months, seasons, weeks
Telling the time
24-hour clock

24-hour clock, calendar, time zones
Calculating periods of time, e.g. duration of lessons, rail timetables, etc.
Time and distance relationships
Simple speed

Pictorial presentation and interpretation

Pictogram (pictures in one-to-one correspondence)
Block Graph (one square to one object): two columns
Block Graph (one square to one object): more than two columns
Block graph
Arrow diagram
Grids — fixing position
Co-ordinates
Deducing facts from graph

Block graph with scale
Simple line graph
Co-ordinates
Mapping and relation

Simple equations
Simple probability
Pie chart
Conversion graph

Graphs of algebraic expressions
Plotting co-ordinates in four quadrants
Simple algebraic terms including negative numbers
Algebraic inequalities (leading to linear programming)
Problems involving equations

Mathematical Profile

NUMBER

NUMBER	Recognises and writes numerals	Orders	Adds with aids	Adds no aids	Subtracts with aids	Subtracts no aids	Multiplies with aids	Multiplies no aids	Divides with aids	Divides no aids
Whole numbers less than 10										
Whole numbers less than 20										
Whole numbers less than 100										
Whole numbers more than 100										
Numbers to 2 decimal places										
Further decimals										
Bases other than 10										
Fractions less than 1										
Mixed numbers										
+ve and −ve numbers										

SHAPE AND SPACE

SHAPE AND SPACE	Recognised and Discussed
Simple 3D and 2D shapes	
Moves of body or object: Balance, turn, slide	
Simple tessellations	
Symmetry: Line	
Rotational	
Plans	
Horizontal and vertical	
Parallels	
Constructions and nets	
Similarity and scale	
Congruence	
Position: Co-ordinates	
Bearings	
Transformation Reflection	
Rotation	
Translation	
Properties: Triangles	
Quadrilaterals	
Regular shapes	
Mensuration:	Can measure

Number facts

Number facts:			
Multiplication tables:	Recalls quickly and can demonstrate if necessary		
	× 2	× 5	× 8
	× 3	× 6	× 9
	× 4	× 7	× 10

Calculates

Calculates	
Averages	
Factors	
H.C.F./L.C.M.	
Percentages	

Alegbra

Alegbra:	
Uses letters to represent simple arithmetic problem	
Substitutes numbers for letters	
Solves simple linear equation	

MEASURES

MEASURES	Compares directly	Orders
Length		
Area		
Vol./cap.		
Mass		
Time		
Angle		

TIME

TIME	Reads from clock	Writes in words	Reads	Writes
O'clock				
Half hour				
Quarter hour				
Minutes				

	Reads and	Writes
Days		
Months		
Seasons		
Dates		

Reads and can use	
Calendar	
a.m. and p.m.	
24 hour clock	
Timetables	

Standard Units

Standard Units:		Sees need for this standard unit	Records mixed units in decimal form in this unit	Uses these related standard units
Length	m			
	cm			
	mm			
	dm			
	km			
Area	m²			
	cm²			
	mm²			
	ha			
Vol./cap.	l			
	ml			
	dm³			
	cm³			
Mass	g			
	kg			
	t			
Time	s			
	min			
	h			
Angle	°			

Perimeter:
- Rectangles
- Compound shapes

Area:
- Rectangles
- Triangles
- Compound shapes
- Surfaces of solids

Volume:
- Cuboids
- Prisms generally
- Cone and pyramid

MONEY

Recognises these coins or notes		
1p	10p	£1
2p	20p	£5
5p	50p	£10

Makes up using other coins		
2p	10p	50p
5p	20p	£1

Shopping:	Totals up to:	Gives change from
20p		
50p		
£1		
£10		
Over £10		

REPRESENTATION

REPRESENTATION	Picto-gram	Block graph	Pie chart	Scatter-gram	Flow chart	Mapp-ings
Draws conclusions from:						
Represents data without help as:						

No record scheme is perfect, and obviously any scheme that is adopted will only be effective if it is regularly completed by each teacher in the school. Unfortunately, all too often record schemes are hastily completed the week before children transfer to the next class. In this situation the record will serve no useful purpose at all.

Profile sheet

As an alternative to the continuous recording of progress some teachers prefer to use a profile sheet as a check of mathematical attainment. Here the profile is completed for a child at a certain time and the information is assumed to indicate the stage of development at that particular time. Sometimes a profile is based on criteria-referenced-type questions. In the example given it is assumed that the teacher will be able to complete the entries against each item by a combination of current knowledge, checking written work and questioning. Profiles like this one are often used on transfer between schools, and they can of course be based on a summary of the stage of development reached on a continuous record scheme.

Incidental assessment

Naturally the teacher will acquire a lot of knowledge about the progress of children in the class through day-to-day contact. This informal kind of assessment is very important. There can be no real substitute for the teacher being involved in an active learning situation incorporating a great deal of discussion with the child. A cassette recorder can be useful in keeping an aural record of this dialogue.

REFERENCES

1. DES, *Mathematics from 5 to 16*, Curriculum Matters 3, An HMI Series (HMSO, 1985).
2. A. Brighouse, D. Godber, P. Patilla, *Mathematics 8 to 12* (NFER-Nelson, 1983).
3. A.N. Hieronymus, E.F. Lindquist, N. France, *Richmond Tests of Basic Skills* (NFER-Nelson, 1974).

4. N. France, *Profile of Mathematical Skills* (NFER-Nelson, 1979).

5. Author Unspecified, *Yardsticks: Criterion-Referenced Tests in Mathematics* (NFER-Nelson, 1977).

6. D. & M.M. Lumb, *Early Mathematics Diagnostic Kit* (NFER-Nelson, 1987).

Appendix

Illustrations of Local Authority Support for Teachers

SOUTH TYNESIDE YOUNG MATHEMATICIAN AWARD SCHEME (STYMAS)

The aim of the scheme is to present a range of mathematical activities not usually directly included in the majority of schemes of work in an award giving package. With the emphasis on being actively involved with the scheme any child can progress to receive the bronze, silver and finally the gold award.

How the scheme works

(1) Activities are placed in clusters of 16, 18 and 18 at the bronze, silver and gold levels respectively. A certificate is awarded when the child has completed all the activities at that level.
(2) An individual record sheet is available for each child. A class record is available for recording the progress for all the children taking part in the scheme.
(3) A set of notes for each level briefly explains each activity for the teacher.
(4) The scheme should be suitable for children from the age of about eight.
(5) There is no time limit for the scheme.
(6) Competition between children is not to be encouraged. The activities are designed so that all children who persevere can progress to the gold level.
(7) The scheme should complement the normal work in the mathematics classroom. Most activities require little or no direct teacher involvement.

(8) The scheme is capable of use in the early secondary years and with children in special schools.

(9) Each completed activity must be signed by the teacher as proof of completion.

Mathematical activities

Bronze level
(1) Drawn 36-point Mystic Rose.
(2) Curve stitched.
(3) Made 20 shapes from tangram.
(4) Tessellated.
(5) Made straw cube, tetrahedron and octahedron.
(6) Calibrated litre container.
(7) Won 3 games of addition football.
(8) Investigated 3×3 and 4×4 magic square.
(9) Made design using basic shapes.
(10) Typed mathematical program.
(11) Read mathematics book.
(12) Investigated square and triangle numbers to 100.
(13) Devised mathematical game.
(14) Followed mathematical trail round school.
(15) Calculated total skin area on body.
(16) Folded conic sections.

Silver level
(1) Found the curves in 20×20 multiplication square.
(2) Drawn ellipse with pins and string.
(3) Made and used Napier's rods.
(4) Mastered finger multiplication.
(5) Made Platonic solids and discovered Euler.
(6) Found cardioid in circle.
(7) Located Mary Rose.
(8) Won three games of division football.
(9) Made measurement scrapbook.
(10) Experimented with M program.
(11) Discovered Sieve of Eratosthenes.
(12) Made hexiflexagon.
(13) Planned excursion.
(14) Produced three origami objects.
(15) Undertaken approved investigation.
(16) Estimated height of building.

(17) Investigated spiral and helix.

(18) Found golden rectangle.

Gold level

(1) Made ruled surface.

(2) Made Soma cube.

(3) Beaten computer at Reversi.

(4) Made dodecahedron from card.

(5) Produced money poster.

(6) Investigated products of 37.

(7) Made set of magic window cards.

(8) Investigated Fibonacci.

(9) Computed in octal system.

(10) Studied Konigsberg Bridges.

(11) Solved rubic cube.

(12) Written short program.

(13) Produced mathematical trail.

(14) Answered questions on mathematical book.

(15) Solved mathematical paradox.

(16) Solved hexagon number problem.

(17) Discovered π.

(18) Used scatter diagram.

A detailed set of notes is available for each level. These give guidance to the teacher with regard to each activity.

Examples of materials available to the teacher

South Tyneside Young Mathematician Award Scheme

GOLD LEVEL CERTIFICATE

Awarded to

_____

at_____ School

Signed *K. Stringer*

Director of Education

<u>STYMAS</u>

Name _____

School _____

<u>GOLD</u>

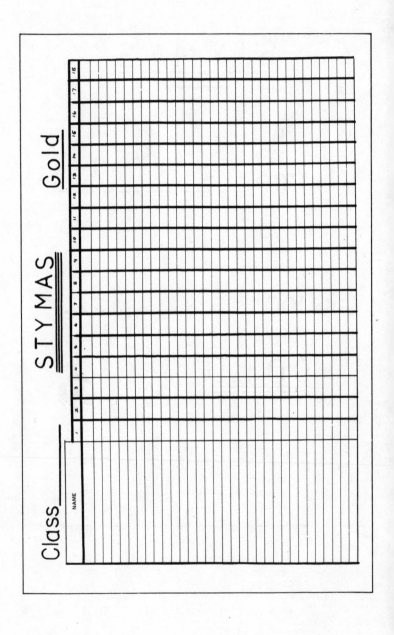

S T Y M A S

<u>Teacher Instructions</u>

<u>Bronze Level</u>

1. Mystic Rose formed by joining each one of 36 (say) equally spaced
    points on circumference of large circle to every other point.

2. Curve stiching is known to most teachers. Child should be
    encouraged to use straight lines and curves. Be imaginative.

3. Standard tangram is made by cutting seven pieces from square
    as shown.

4. Tessellation (fitting shapes together to make a pattern) can
    be done with both regular and irregular shapes.

5. Three dimensional straw modelling can be done using plasticine
    for corners or small pieces of pipe cleaner.

6. Calibration can be done using small containers. Pop bottles are
    ideal. Do not worry too much if child uses $1\frac{1}{2}$ litre or 2 litre
    container.

7. Addition football is attached. Extra copies can be obtained
    from Teachers' Centre or D. Lumb directly. Games should be with
    other members of class.

8. This is an example of a 3 x 3 magic square.
    The total for each row, each column and each
    diagonal is the same. The example is a
    "normal" magic square because it makes use of
    consecutive whole numbers starting from 1.

8	1	6
3	5	7
4	9	2

MATHEMATICAL TRAILS

Most schemes of work in primary schools aim to make children
aware of mathematics in their environment, and much useful
work tends to be done using the school as the focal point. The
aim of the trail is to provide an opportunity for children to
undertake similar work in any urban or rural centre. Schools
may of course develop their own trails in the vicinity of the
school.

APPENDIX

Choice of area

The area chosen for a trail must be one which interests the children and be worthy of investigation. The choice here was part of old Newcastle near to the Quayside containing the castle, cathedral, River Tyne, bridges, busy roads, fine buildings and a church but possessing safe walking for the children. Although many of the children knew the area, few had actually visited it.

It is essential in the planning of trails to include access to toilet facilities, and also remember that materials such as paper, pencils, clipboards, etc., will be needed.

Age range

The original intention was to produce one trail for the infant child and one for the junior child but problems of language and concern for safety resulted in the decision not to progress with the infant trail. The *First Maths Trail* has been designed for children in the eight-to-nine age range and the *Second Maths Trail* for those in the ten-to-twelve age range, although the teacher would need to choose the trail most suited to the pupils in the group. Each trail should take about two hours to complete but can be taken in parts if the teacher wishes.

Presentation

The trails are presented to the child in booklet form. It is essential that whatever form of presentation is chosen, the product is lively, interesting, and well written. The trail reproduced here is the one produced for the younger children and uses three different stopping places where the children gather their information.

Preparation

Teachers should familiarise themselves with the content of the booklet beforehand and preferably take a walk along the trail if at all possible. It is most important that the children should

138

understand the terminology used so that no time is wasted on the trail. It is also advisable that the mathematical skills used during the trail are explained and practised in school prior to the visit. By doing this, problems (such as 'Which category does a van fit into?') can be discussed and decided on beforehand.

Problems for later

Each booklet contains 'problems for later' which ask the child to gather some information and use it later. These assignments will require more time than will be available when following the trail and should be tackled back in the classroom. This enables follow-up work to be undertaken by the teacher.

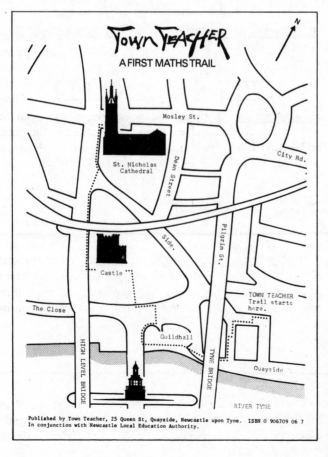

Published by Town Teacher, 25 Queen St, Quayside, Newcastle upon Tyne. ISBN 0 906709 06 7
In conjunction with Newcastle Local Education Authority.

Pages from the Trails

1. The Swing Bridge. (Standing on the Swing Bridge).

Tick the bridges you can see.

Look at each of the first four bridges in turn.

If the bridge is used by motor vehicles put the letter M in the box below the picture. If it is used by trains put the letter T and if it is used by pedestrians put the letter P.

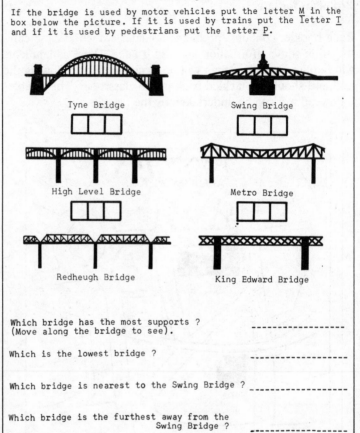

Which bridge has the most supports ?
(Move along the bridge to see).

_____

Which is the lowest bridge ?

_____

Which bridge is nearest to the Swing Bridge ? _____

Which bridge is the furthest away from the
                        Swing Bridge ?

_____

1.

2 . Castle Garth .

Draw the well as if looking from above.

Mark in the various stones.

Are all the stones the same size ?

How many children need to hold
hands to make a close circle
around the well ?(Stretch out
your arms as far as possible.)

You have now measured the
<u>circumference</u> of the outside
of the well.

Measure the circumference

a) in handspans,

b) in footlengths.

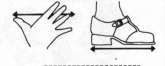

> PROBLEM FOR LATER COMPARE THE MEASUREMENTS YOU MADE OF THE
> CIRCUMFERENCE WITH THOSE OF YOUR FRIENDS. ARE THEY THE SAME?
> IF NOT, WHY NOT?

Look at the Keep.

How old do you think this
building is ?

When was the building of the
present Keep completed ?

> PROBLEM FOR LATER WORK OUT
> HOW OLD THE KEEP IS.
> HOW NEAR WAS YOUR ESTIMATE?

The Keep is 27 metres high.

Look at the Bridge Hotel.

Estimate it's height.

3.

141

MAGAZINES

Many authorities produced short magazines to provide extra stimulus for the children. The examples have been found very useful with children between the ages of eight and thirteen and are taken from *Prism* magazine.

UZZLES

IDDLES

NVESTIGATIONS

EQUENCES

ATHEMATICS

SPRING TERM 1986   ISSUE 1

5. DOUBLETS.

Lewis Carroll (author of Alice in Wonderland)
published a collection of "Doublets". As an example
he showed how to turn HEAD into TAIL by altering one
letter at a time, with the least number of links.
   e.g. HEAD - HEAL - TEAL - TELL - TALL - TAIL
Try these -
a)   PIG into STY.
b)   TEARS into SMILE.
c)   APE into OWL.
d)   WHIG INTO TORY.
e)   SHIP into DOCK.
f)   COAL into MINE.

ARCHERY PUZZLE.

How many arrows does it take to score exactly
100 on this target?

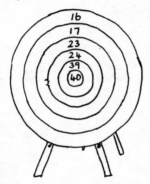

ST. IVES.

As I was going to St. Ives,
I met a man with seven wives,
Every wife had seven sacks,
Every sack had seven cats,
Every cat had seven kits,
Kits, cats, sacks, and wives,
How many were there going to St. Ives?

TESSELLATIONS.

Everyone is familiar with tessellations made with squares or rectangles from the tile patterns on kitchen floors and on brickwork, but can you make tessellations with sets of other shapes of quadrilateral shown below?

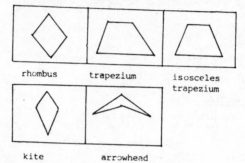

rhombus   trapezium   isosceles
                          trapezium

kite   arrowhead

HOW MANY COINS?

A man changed a number of £1 coins into 5p and 10p coins, and received six more 5p coins than 10p coins. What is the smallest number of £1 coins changed, and how many of each coin did the man receive?

On another occasion he changed £12 and again was given 6 more 5p coins than 10p coins. How many coins did he receive?

CHESS BOARD PATTERN.

The black squares shown are those which can be reached in one move by a knight in the central square of a 5 x 5 mini chess board. Find the pattern made by the squares that can be reached in a minimum of a) two moves, b) three moves.

Index